# THE
# TITANIUM
# PROFESSIONAL

# THE
# TITANIUM
# PROFESSIONAL

Building EXCITING, RESILIENT and DURABLE careers
through the power of INDEPENDENT capability

# HUGH DAVIES

Business & Professional Publishing

Business + Publishing
Unit 7/5 Vuko Place
Warriewood NSW 2102
Australia
ACN 054 568 688
Email: info@bpp.com.au
Website: www.bpp.com.au

First published 2000
Reprinted 2000

National Library of Australia
Cataloguing-in-Publication data
Davies, Hugh, 1945-.
    Titanium Professional: Building exciting and resilient careers.
    Bibliography.
    ISBN 1 875680 85 3.
    1. Career development. I. Title.

370.113

Publisher: Tim Edwards
Cover by: Liz Seymour
Printed in Australia by the Australian Print Group
Business + Publishing is an imprint of Business and Professional Publishing Pty Ltd.

Distributed in Australia and New Zealand by Woodslane Pty Ltd. Business + Publishing titles are available through booksellers and other resellers. For further information contact Woodslane Australia on +61 2 9970 5111 or Woodslane Ltd, New Zealand on +64 6 347 6543, or email info@bpp.com.au.

# Contents

## Chapter 4

## Chapter 5

## Chapter 6

## Chapter 7

# *Preface*

We set off into our working lives, or into new jobs when changing employment, with a variety of aspirations. We generally want to be successful, earn good salaries, learn new skills and abilities and have great relationships with others.

However, when we look around us, succeeding at work and achieving these things independently appears to be well nigh impossible — or at least limited by all sorts of barriers. Succeeding at work often appears to require submerging one's individuality, being 'ground down' with work pressure or having to play politics in an organisation. Threats of constant technological change, of organisational restructurings and downsizings also loom. However, we do see success stories around us, so we should be asking *how* to steer a successful path.

How can we reconcile the contradictions these issues present and achieve a measure of success, fulfilment and fun in our working lives and also ensure that all our other interests are met as well? Life should be about being fulfilled in relationships, about having a fund of stories for one's grandchildren and being satisfied in the expression of our talents — yet the pressures and trade-offs for succeeding at work seem altogether opposed to these ambitions.

The realities of modern economics and technology mean that organisations and corporations will continue to exist — with changes we will be discussing — and most of us will need to work in an organisation for much of our working lives. The outcomes required of most of our professions and managerial jobs will still need to be delivered in the future. Accountants will still need to produce financial data, achieve compliance with reporting requirements, and undertake analyses. Marketers will continue to appraise opportunities and formulate strategy — and so, in turn, will other professions continue into the future.

It isn't usually an option for us to head off to an ashram or live off the land. And if our tastes and desires require a reasonable income, we will have to work quite hard to attain worthwhile positions. When we look around at what 'work' is becoming for many people — when we see its effects in pressured, distorted personalities, people displaced from organisations due to restructuring and feeling *sorry* for themselves — it seems that something is seriously wrong in our society. Have we become captive to an array of conventions, values and behaviours which are exacting a terrible price?

A price is certainly there to be seen in stressed, tense, highly focused people, in the absence of time for relationships, in organisational 'politics' and in the 'hurry sickness' all around us. It is to be seen in the elevation of people with nicknames like 'Chainsaw', in the absence of ethical standards in some business leaders, in the periodic retrenchment of long-serving staff from organisations and in the anxiety in those who remain. It is evident in the elevation of short-term shareholder returns over the creation of customer and staff loyalty; it is evident in the absence of trust and warmth within many organisations.

Can we head into work in the future without succumbing to this multiplicity of diseases and unpleasant consequences? Can we be independent and capable, working within the environments of organisations in the future, without being changed or ground down, without losing our decency or a comfortable sense of ourselves? Can we work hard without becoming hard? Can we achieve great things, for ourselves and the organisations we are within, without being caught up on a treadmill? Can we become a 'titanium professional'?

We can and that is what this book is about.

We can find professional satisfaction without recourse to power dressing, without learning the art of corporate assassination and without becoming an 80-hour-a-week slave to pressure. We can grow internally in the course of our work.

This is not a book about creating better organisations — leaner fighting machines. Nor is it a book about becoming hard-edged, aggressive or more 'noticed' than the next person in the corporate jungle.

Increasingly, young entrants to the workplace are rejecting the practices and organisational cultures of the last decade or so of management. They are selecting different environments, or quietly moving on after a period of learning in some of the less attractive organisations. Increasingly, those who are displaced at later stages in their careers are choosing new and different paths for themselves — but often doing so with a sense of regret that their 'lost' years won't be recoverable.

Of course, not all organisations are 'jungles' where only the fittest survive. Some offer a collegial atmosphere and an absence of unnecessary hierarchy. There are some with great communications, opportunity for individual empowerment, an infectious focus on customers and time for fun as well as work. They are usually small, or are small autonomous groups within larger organisations, but these environments are few and far between.

There are other reasons for developing independent capability. 'Work' as such is changing within most professions. Some forms of work are disappearing altogether and new occupations are emerging. With these and many other influences which will be discussed, the case for managing your own career, or your various careers, is becoming stronger by the day.

And while work is changing, organisations and the way in which activities are co-ordinated in manufacturing and services are also changing. So we need to address the skills and talents that help us achieve an independent capability — not so much in the organisations of the past, but for those emerging in the future.

*The Titanium Professional* is about developing independent capability — a set of competencies that deliver both success in work and the adventures and fulfilment which all of us need in achieving great lives.

## Why the 'titanium professional'?

A strong metaphor forms the title of this book. This is a book for professionals — for people who set out to grow their careers around one or more fields of expertise. It is also a book for those who seek a measure of resilience and inner strength within themselves. And this is where 'titanium' comes in. Titanium is a strong, durable, unscratchable metal which does not wear easily. It has low elastic modulus, to use a technical term. That is, it does not dent easily and quickly 'springs back' after impact — one reason it is used in spectacle frames and in golf clubs.

The premise of this book is that we should set out to build a resilient, durable, independent capability in fashioning and guiding our own careers — we should set out to become 'titanium professionals' in our working lives. Here's how.

# Acknowledgements

Books like this one invariably reflect the insights of a great many people — not simply those of one author. I hope I have sufficiently acknowledged the influences of authors such as Daniel Goleman, Stephen Covey, Noel Turnbull and many others in the text itself. Here I want to acknowledge the support of friends and colleagues whose ideas and responses have contributed to this work.

First and foremost of these is my wife, Sheila, whose skills in editing and in spotting logic chasms helped immensely in getting this book to the point where it was be readable.

I would also like to acknowledge my two sons, Michael and Andrew, who in early adulthood have become sources of all sorts of advice and inspiration to their father.

Next, I need to thank Tim Edwards, of Business & Professional Publishing, who used the publication of an article of mine to contact me and prompt me into taking on this larger project. Tim has supported me patiently with suggestions and continuing enthusiasm through the whole period involved in getting *The Titanium Professional* to publication.

I must also acknowledge those who agreed to be case studies in this book: Trevor Sinclair, Susan Holmes, Paul McKessy, Yolanda Pettinato, Richard Panelli, Steve Adamek, Ian Greenshields and Frank Whitford. I am immensely grateful for the inspiration each provided, for their patience in being interviewed and for their agreement to have a small measure of their lives exposed in this book. Since the text of this book was written Frank's circumstances have changed; the organisation which he led has now been dismantled and its constituent business sold to new owners. However this is a book about individuals – not about organisations – and I look forward to hearing about the next career Frank decides to create for himself.

Finally, there are a great many friends, and current and past colleagues, whose guidance needs mention. Of course, I cannot cover them all, but I would particularly like to thank Frederick Davidson, Chair of RightD&A (formally Davidson & Associates), for all that he has taught me about career transition counselling, and my other colleagues in this organisation, who provide such a terrific and collegial environment. I am especially grateful in this context for the wisdom of Judith Cougle and the enthusiasm of Maggie Gloster.

Beyond this group, I thank Richard Curtain for a continuing stream of wisdom, Tom Valenta — another early 'encourager' in the idea of writing this book — and Ros McCarthy in the UK for her enthusiastic support.

Tom, Ian, Judith, Ros and Susan were also kind enough to read and critique the first draft of this book, and for this I owe them all another big thank you.

# *chapter one*

## Why be independently capable?

Being employed in some form of work is a significant focus in our education and preparation for becoming independent adults. Work will take us to a new plateau in growth, maturity and financial independence.

However, workplace change is becoming increasingly apparent. As we seek out self-definition and fulfilment at work, the activity itself seems to be a shifting target. Change is constantly occurring in the things we call 'work', in organisational arrangements, in where work is to be found, and even in how we are paid.

## 'Work' is changing shape

Work isn't diminishing, but it is changing significantly. We see organisations being restructured, downsized, merged and sold. Government organisations are being corporatised, privatised and then also sold. Jobs are being transformed and a lot of work is now done by those without tenured positions.

Plenty of books and articles address the subject of organisational change. Organisations are exhorted to refashion themselves to meet the challenges of competition, become better leaders, trim costs and become lean, create and sustain better cultures, become more customer-driven, and so on. Since organisational change often results in people being displaced, inevitably much of what we read is about coping with this adverse consequence. Change itself can be threatening, and much of what we read is overlaid with pessimism and messages about how to 'survive'.

Certainly, professionals do need the skills to deal with unplanned career change — but *The Titanium Professional* is about capturing *opportunities* in the future world of work. It is a book about *individuals*, not organisations. It is about how *you* can find growth and fulfilment in work when all around you is changing so much.

Some of the books about change in work and its implication for careers are excellent. Charles Handy has been writing books — including *The Age of Unreason* and *The Empty Raincoat* — about new work paradigms in the next generation of organisations for several years. *Jobshift*, by William Bridges, and *We Are All Self-employed*, by

Cliff Hakim, also present thought-provoking reading.

Individual professionals clearly need to learn some new skills, to become differently equipped, in order to grow in employability in the shifting environments of the future. Like seasoned travellers preparing for new expeditions, like guerrilla fighters moving through jungles and adapting to our environment, we need to become both independent and capable in the very different working world of the future. We must move beyond merely understanding the changing picture of organisations and work towards being *independently capable* in such contexts.

How is this going to be possible? If people are well into their careers, how can they build more certainty into their future employment and growth, when so much of the change in organisations (and in work itself) seems beyond their control?

This book addresses ways in which individuals become independently capable within the context of all the changes affecting work. First, however, let us examine the ways in which independent capability is becoming so important. What are the trends that Handy, Bridges, Hakim and others are writing about?

## Seven reasons for becoming independently capable

There are seven trends to see and understand: seven reasons for becoming independently capable.

### 1    Work within jobs is changing.

We need to fashion the skills and abilities which turn these changes into opportunities.

### 2    'Jobs' are disappearing.

The job we have today may not be here tomorrow. We need to see work as an evolving series of activities and to understand that defined jobs in settled organisations are but one vehicle of employment.

### 3    Industries are changing and sometimes moving offshore.

Our careers, then, ought not to be industry specific and may be built on the opportunities created by globalisation.

**4    Organisations are downsizing and outsourcing work.**

New opportunities, especially in service niches, are continually evolving.

**5    Organisations are changing their structures.**

Increasingly, they are using contingent arrangements and alliances with others to achieve their outcomes.

**6    You are your own best career coach.**

Despite the good intentions of some organisations, generally we will do a better job than our organisations in managing our own career development.

**7    You are changing.**

You can drive changes in your work to fit your inner needs and growth rather than expect organisations to match the timing of your changes.

Let us examine these reasons for developing independent capability in more detail.

**Work within jobs is changing**

The three key drivers of change within jobs are technology, customers and knowledge. It can be difficult to distinguish between these influences, but we can look at some broad examples.

In recent years, computer literacy has become a requirement common to almost all jobs. But there have also been changes specific to particular fields of work, driven by technology and changes in knowledge or approaches within the work.

Within the finance professions, for example, new approaches to shareholder value measurement, new forms of investment and risk management, and new business structures and joint venture arrangements demand continual change and development among professionals. Externally, changes in accounting procedures, taxation legislation and company reporting standards, and compliance requirements also affect the nature of work.

The same story applies in any profession, including human resource management, marketing or operations management. Continuing practice of the same skills and knowledge, even in established and well-defined professions such as medicine and teaching, is increasingly impossible to sustain.

Medicine is clearly affected by ongoing discoveries in treatment regimes and in drug usage. For example, the combination of non-invasive surgical technologies, severe cost pressures in the health system and new approaches to ambulatory care has transformed a patient's length of stay in hospital — and at the same time has had a major impact on surgeons, nursing staff and paramedical staff. Many more medical and surgical procedures are
now performed on a day–treatment basis and when a hospital bed is required, patients are now on their way home much quicker than before. More use is made of home visits by paramedical staff. Reception staff are being benchmarked against best practice in hotel reception practices to improve patient admission efficiency and to use information technologies more effectively.

Secondary and tertiary teaching is another profession undergoing change. It is being strongly influenced by the information revolution, by distance learning, by new approaches to collaboration among students and project work — and by a focus on broad competencies in conjunction with fields of knowledge such as mathematics and chemistry. These interests have sometimes displaced a necessary concurrent focus on the three Rs — but they are increasingly seen as new and critical skill combinations. Some of the broader competencies now promoted by educationalists are particularly relevant to our search for independent capability at work — and we'll return to these later.

As customers require more speed, better quality, new features, and more comprehensive and responsive service, so our work must change. From direct debit facilities in supermarkets to Internet share trading — the world is changing rapidly, and consumers are keeping pace. Financial planners must now offer much more sophisticated and detailed advice to a well-informed customer base, and now to a growing market of people operating do-it-yourself superannuation funds.

All jobs are changing like this: the initial vocational skill development for most working roles is simply the first platform of professional learning. Increasingly we must look to education as a process which teaches people how to learn, rather than one which is merely about imparting information.

Not only is work within existing professions changing, but *new* work is emerging, bringing with it new professions. In this arena we see designers of web pages and organisations which help others capture commercial value from the Internet. We see new specialisations in medicine and the law — one of which is a growing focus on the management of intellectual capital. We see new businesses emerging, delivering a wide array of services to the homes of busy working couples. New work is all around us, and we will look at this a little more in Chapter 3.

### 'Jobs' are disappearing

As William Bridges observes in *Jobshift*, while the demand for work in a widening variety of forms continues, the 'job' is disappearing: 'Work will not be contained in the familiar envelopes we call jobs'.[1]

A primary driver of this restructuring is the impact of technology and the information revolution. Computer-aided design and robotics are changing manufacturing processes. The Internet is changing communication systems. Software systems in the fields of design, logistics, word-processing and publishing, to mention just a few examples, are replacing whole fields of work. The demise of the secretary/typist is well advanced. Conductors and guards on trains and trams, bookkeepers, design draughtspeople and whole layers of middle managers are disappearing.

But if 'jobs' are disappearing, is work disappearing too? Not at all! New work, as described and as emerging in the growing numbers of self-employed people, is all around us. Independently capable people seek and sustain rewarding work in a variety of settings where a job on someone else's payroll is incidental, not essential.

---

[1] William Bridges, *Jobshift*, Allen & Unwin, Sydney, 1994, p.viii.

## Industries are changing

Industries are changing and parts of them are even disappearing or being 'moved' offshore. Vehicle manufacturing plants become assembly plants for components manufactured elsewhere. Broad-based manufacturing centres become specialist operations, making perhaps doors or engines, for shipment all over the world. As this occurs, occupations in one or another country disappear, or are significantly changed.

But new work and new opportunities emerge in the wake of these shifts. The new work may involve logistics, communications and new skills in the assessment of taxation environments in different countries, in new financial instruments and in international trade arrangements.

While one multinational company may close down a manufacturing plant in one country and centralise production of components in another, professional accounting firms are hiring increasing numbers of people for work in international finance, in mergers and acquisition advisory work and in expatriate tax management, to support the international operations.

Years ago I had a minor role reviewing trades training programs for the Singaporean government. The issues being addressed by what was then a very young country included thinking about how tradespeople should be trained and how far the government should go in replicating the practices of Western countries with seasoned traditions in trades training.

I made a review of trades training practices in the United Kingdom and of centres where groups of companies pooled their expenditure on training costs to provide excellent workshops, instructors and curricula for tradespeople in training. The centres had certainly improved former traditions around apprenticeship development and the end result, in one example, equipped graduating fitters and turners with the skill to take a lump of raw steel and fashion beautifully turned out pulley wheels and sheaves.

However the reality was that many of these superbly skilled young tradespeople were then employed in vehicle assembly lines, guiding computer-controlled robotic equipment and using a fraction of the skills previously taught.

Needless to say, Singapore fashioned a series of technician training programs much more aligned with the needs of industry and the people choosing this career entry path.

## Organisations are downsizing

We have experienced nearly a decade of downsizing, where companies reduce staff numbers in divisions or operations which are seen as unattractive, or perhaps where centralisation of functions is occurring.

In the period 1993–95, 44 percent of organisations in Australia 'de-layered', and middle managers were the primary target of the cuts.[2] In a survey of 1008 managers in outplacement programs, some questions focused on the reasons for the last five career changes made by the respondents. Interestingly, employer–initiated moves such as restructuring and retrenchment rose as the reason for the most recent job change from 14 percent in earlier years to 37 percent.[3]

There can be good reasons for these trends, as organisations strive to create more agile, flexible business operations. There can also be poor reasons for downsizing, where short–term accounting measures of returns offer more appeal in a boardroom than the alternative — encouraging growth through more astute marketing or through product development. More often than not, key operational history, knowledge and disciplines 'walk out the door' in the name of rationalisation. Some of those who research company performances over time are questioning the real costs and the failure of promised benefits in companies that have downsized in the past few years.

Fred Reichfield, author of *The Loyalty Effect*, was quoted by Colleen Ryan in 1998:

*The average company loses half its customers in five years, half its employees*

---

[2] C. R. Littler, T. Bramble and R. Dunford, 'Downsizing: a Disease or a Cure.' in *HR Monthly*, August 1996, pp. 8–12.
[3] T. Marchant, R. Critchley and C. Littler, 'Managers on the Move.' in *HR Monthly*, October 1997, pp. 6–8.

*in four years and half its investors in less than one year. People don't understand the devastating costs of churn. We seem to face a future in which the only business relationships will be opportunistic transactions between virtual strangers...*[4]

Is this where we are headed? Or are we in a phase of organisational evolution, after which all the weaknesses of this period will be recognised?

We can attack ruthless downsizing — with its focus on cost-cutting and building short-term shareholder returns — and ask whether focus on customers and opportunities for growth might amount to a better strategy. Alternatively, we can learn to have different expectations of our employers. We can set out to limit our dependence on positions in organisations and look for new work and new *opportunities* in the areas of change we've examined.

We can be resilient and more durable than the organisations through which we move.

## Organisations are changing their structures

Organisations now routinely outsource 'non-core' functions such as recruitment, accounting and auditing, property and facilities management, information systems design, procurement and maintenance, some aspects of marketing (such as telemarketing), legal advice and process, public affairs and issues management, training, and even strategy assessment and the acquisition and divestment of operations. The words 'non-core' are in inverted commas above, because it is sometimes difficult to see what is 'core' and what is not!

Large, vertically integrated companies are breaking up into smaller businesses and new shared services (such as call centres) are providing customer contact processes for multiple-client organisations. Specialist niche operators are emerging. At the same time, alliances or networks are developing between them, and with the larger organisations being

---

[4] Colleen Ryan, 'It seemed like a good idea.' *Australian Financial Review*, 17 January, 1998, p. 25.

built on rapidly evolving services and technologies. If this is what is coming, maybe there is a brighter upside to current organisational change.

Charles Handy has been writing about the changing structures of organisational life and anticipating these trends for many years. However, his predictions of a move to smaller corporate centres and wholesale outsourcing to different layers of contracted agencies are being proved correct faster than even he might have envisaged.

Outsourcing naturally displaces jobs and work within organisations, but it creates work as well — within the new specialist operations set up to receive outsourced work contracts. For a time, at least, the implications include a growth of new jobs in smaller, specialist organisations and the disappearance of the breadth of experience large organisations were able to provide previously.

One new professional field to emerge from these processes is outplacement or career transition consulting: the business of helping displaced employees successfully design and achieve a new career. Incidentally, this field of work is one of the two new careers I have adopted following some 30 years as a human resource manager. I now have two part-time jobs rather than one full-time job, making me one of an increasing number of people adopting 'portfolio careers' (that is, portfolios of activities) as Charles Handy terms them.

Work is increasingly contract or project based for many people. In his book, *We Are All Self-employed,* Cliff Hakim uses the description 'contingent employment' to describe this phenomenon—where work is required and paid for by organisations, but no permanent, full-time employment relationship is put in place.[5] New 'professions' as contract managers are emerging—along with 'systems implementers', 'manufacturing facility builders' and 'divesters of businesses'. The people who take on this work are building on a platform of professional experience and training, fulfilling defined contracts with a stream of organisations — albeit with the risk of discontinuity in employment.

---

[5] C. Hakim, *We Are All Self-employed*, Berrett-Koehler Publishers, San Francisco, 1994.

In *Making Your Future Work*, Marcus Letcher identifies the range of contingent roles emerging:

- task work
- project work
- casual work
- part-time work
- contract work — both independent and via agencies
- fee-for-service positions
- consultancy
- contingent — as required — work
- sessional positions
- fixed-term contracts.[6]

By world standards, Australia's reliance on part-time and casual work is extraordinary, exceeded in the Organisation for Economic Co-operation and Development (OECD) nations only by Spain. In the past 14 years the proportion of employees working part-time has risen by eight percent and by August 1999 represented 26 percent of the number of those employed.[7]

Clearly, the trends described here show a different view of the employment relationship emerging. As Hakim observes,

*…the familiar employer – employee contract has now been broken: loyalty to the organisation no longer guarantees job security.*[8]

Whereas employers used to celebrate loyalty, tenure and service, now much more weight is given to skills, competencies and the current needs of the organisation and its market. The notion that an organisation is itself a community, containing within it a need to develop and nourish community values, now seems to have limited appeal.

For many years I was the Director of Personnel and Corporate Affairs in an Australian multinational. It was an organisation with a proud 100-year history and many traditions, but during

---

[6] Marcus Letcher, *Making Your Future Work*, Pan Macmillan, Sydney, 1997.
[7] *Australian Financial Review*, 11 April 1997; 'Labour Force Australia', Australian Bureau of Statistics Catalogue 6203.0, August 1999.
[8] Hakim, p xiii.

reorganisation, downsizing of head office functions and some 'clearing of the decks', following the dismissal of its Managing Director, my job was abolished. One of my lesser duties, in the week following this announcement, was to determine (with difficulty) who might be willing to take over the chairperson's role in one of the state-based 25-year service clubs. It was an ironic and difficult task, undertaken within what had become a climate of some fear and distrust in the organisation.

We can rail against these things and join those who deplore the loss of community values in organisations — and we should — but there is another reality, too. This is the need for all of us to develop capabilities which make us independent and mobile in the face of such developments. In these circumstances, we need the characteristics of titanium: we need to be impervious and durable.

*The Titanium Professional* is not about the decline of humanity in corporate life and the reassessment of what might attract and retain greater levels of competence and growth in companies, but about *independent* growth in these environments.

In the light of the foregoing, we should all be counselling our children to expect and plan for several career changes in their lifetimes, and to be ready for at least one of these to be an involuntary change. Learning how to learn, and acquiring the competencies associated with being independently capable, is a big part of our children's development, and fostering these abilities is now a primary responsibility of parenthood.

Of course, many corporations do develop their staff and foster career development. However, even if you are employed by one of these organisations, there is still a strong argument for becoming independently capable.

### You are your own best career coach

Even where others want to help, you can do a better job in your own career development. With the best of intentions, human resource professionals have been developing systems and programs in succession planning and performance appraisal for decades. The truth is that most of these programs really don't work very well. They tend to be driven from the top down, with all the inherent risks of nepotism and of managers looking for people 'like themselves' to promote, instead of looking for people better suited to the very different environments and challenges of the future. Instead of working with the particular energies and enthusiasms of employees, the processes have been made overly bureaucratic.

To be fair, some organisations are now approaching staff development in a more perceptive, holistic fashion. They are much more open and thoughtful about the capabilities they need to develop, and their staff are supported in building their careers independently. Given that these organisations are in the minority, however, and that many organisations are still caught in the approaches of the past, a safe bet is to focus on being independently capable even if the messages about staff development in your organisation sound pretty good. Even organisations committed to staff growth and development are themselves taken over or merged, creating unplanned redundancies.

**You are changing**
The final major reason for developing robust independent capability in your professional life is that each of us develops different sets of aspirations as we develop in our careers and grow older. We are typically establishing skills and an understanding of work in our twenties, in our thirties we are beginning to influence our environment and to manage our professional impact. We then consolidate and reach a career plateau in our forties, and look to perhaps seek more external rewards — to have an impact beyond the workplace — in our fifties. Some people, it seems, have an accelerated path through these transitions, but irrespective of our timing, most of us do move through these broad phases.

This generalisation blends a number of cycles and processes: career and professional maturation, the different phases of adulthood and the necessity to repeat these steps in truncated form as we change careers along the way. It is a generalisation which some might question, but the broad point is that we do change within as the years pass.

We ought not to be trapped in one job through all of these phases. Ideally, we ought to be able to change our work, to manage transitions (rather than have them managed for us) in moving to new careers through a working lifetime.

My grandfather completed a distinguished career as Chief Pathologist at the Royal Children's Hospital in Melbourne, aged 65. At least, this was the expectation of those around him! However, my grandfather asked if he could continue, perhaps in a senior research role, stepping aside to allow a younger aspirant the Chief Pathologist's role. The hospital accepted this proposition with alacrity, and for many years he continued effectively as the senior research fellow to whom difficult cases requiring more considered analysis were referred. He moved to a part-time basis in his seventies and finally stopped work near 80 years old, when he was physically too frail to continue. Throughout this period he remained mentally alert, with a Latin quotation for most occasions. Here was someone in charge of his own career and managing transitions to complement his own changing needs.

By contrast, some people become trapped in the extraordinary pressures of the hours they work and other broader demands. Partners in substantial legal firms, for example, typically generate their own work in relationships with major corporations and other clients. This occurs in a competitive environment in which new work and billable hours are a measure of success. Many face quite extraordinary pressures to attract and retain clients. They are expected to 'play hard' as well as work hard, entertaining clients, hosting functions outside normal hours and the like.

Many people in these situations are somewhat driven with stressed, 'tight' patterns of speech and short attention spans mixed in with the machismo and external insignia of great professional success. They are people whose emotions and feelings have been subordinated to an absolute focus on the tasks, skills and practices which deliver success in their particular organisations or professions. Some professional 'pipelines' in the current work environment are incredibly demanding and not particularly accommodating to the more natural progressions we ought to be able to make as we grow older.

Increasingly, young adults fashioning careers for themselves are rejecting the assumptions and values of these organisational cultures.

Those who work with people displaced by organisational restructuring are often in a position to observe remarkable transformations. Some people have been trapped (sometimes unconsciously, often for years at a time) in quite the wrong jobs. Even involuntary removal of this circumstance lifts a great weight from the individual's shoulders. There is often a positive side to being retrenched. 'Grey', tired people become brighter and much more energetic while working through career change. In essence, the discovery is: I now have an opportunity (thanks in part to a sum of money usually attached to the unpleasant event of job loss) to design and achieve a much better next career! And sometimes another reaction follows: What I find difficult at the moment is all my acquaintances expressing regret at this event, when I'm feeling terrific!

Sometimes the new work which emerges, in all of the restructuring and outsourcing activity, is actually more enjoyable and fulfilling than the previous job. Retrenched and displaced people have often built new and even financially more rewarding 'next' careers through these opportunities. Many have grasped the realities of the way 'work' is now delivered and fashioned well-remunerated activity for themselves without seeking regular employment. Chapter 9 discusses how self-employment and new forms of work can be realised and, with careful management, prove liberating for many people.

## Summary

There are seven key reasons for setting out to be independently capable. The first five refer to the external environment and the last two to ourselves as individuals:

- What we do at work is changing, and we need to keep up with these changes.
- Jobs, as such, are disappearing — we cannot anchor our career around any one 'job' anymore.
- Industries are changing, and new ones are emerging.
- Organisations are changing their structures and the way they operate.

- Each of us, as individuals, can generally be better mentors over our career development than others can be.
- And we are changing too, as we get older.

We should continuously develop the skills, aptitudes and attitudes that prevent us becoming trapped in any one organisation or role. Notions of job security need to be replaced with the idea of career security. We need to develop independent capability in managing career changes and transitions.

Being independently capable does not mean building a suit of armour for protection against unfriendly forces and actions. It is, in part, a process for capturing new opportunities, and for becoming the cause of your own experience.

In *We Are All Self-employed*, Cliff Hakim argues the case for developing and practising a 'self-employed' attitude even within regular corporate environments. He asserts that this can be liberating rather than selfish. It is a philosophy for success.

*The Titanium Professional* is about building the competencies which allow us to achieve this liberating outcome in the emerging world of work.

# *chapter two*

## What is independent capability?

We have seen them about us: people who are unfazed by surprises, unharassed by stressful events; people who seem to have an innate capability to manage themselves in any situation. Some are leaders of others, some are simply self-contained professionals in one field or another. There is no sense about them that they are 'caught up' in the structure of an organisation. Rather, they give the impression that their position is part of a plan — for as long as it can contribute to their interests.

Can we nail down what they possess and acquire some of this ability ourselves?

There are also those who capture 'new work' opportunities: people managing new businesses and those new services that simply did not pass into our awareness as we toiled through the tertiary education system. 'Where did this talent come from?' you ask yourself. 'How on earth did this person learn about this new field, and then capture the opportunity? I don't remember this person as the brightest in the class, by a long shot!'

For many years, educationalists and perceptive employers have understood that success in most forms of work hinges on much more than raw intelligence, or IQ in academic terms. If we are to be independently capable, we had better learn something about what this mystery factor is!

Most of us, of course, have an awareness of skills beyond IQ, but often we aren't good at conceptualising or verbalising them. In this chapter, we define the underlying competencies which are fundamental to success — success, that is, in attaining independent capability. In later chapters, we will look at how to build or improve these competencies.

## What do we really learn at school

Some of the genesis for strong sports programs in schools and the veneration of sporting greats in the community came from the view that schools were a place to 'build character' as well as to prepare young people for academic and career achievement. Schools have long recognised that they exist to develop more than high IQ among their charges.

We have all known exceptionally bright people who excelled at school, but who in later life never seemed to realise the potential we all thought existed in them as young people. At work, we have seen gifted financial analysts, technicians or perhaps information technology experts start well but seem to peak at an early age — and then be passed over for promotion. And we have seen others, not nearly so bright in a technical sense, rise and rise, becoming leaders and divisional heads.

Is the skill of those who do get promoted just being good at politics, or at manipulation, or is something else at work?

The answer is certainly not conspiracy or favouritism, except perhaps occasionally. It is that the possession of key *underlying competencies* is much more fundamental to success in most careers than intelligence as measured in an academic sense.

Many schools are now becoming more discerning and focusing on building broad competencies — going well beyond simply having a strong sporting tradition — in delivering a more rounded education. In fact, based largely on a dialogue between the Australian government and the Business Council of Australia in the late 1980s and early 1990s, a major investigation was initiated into the poor fit then perceived to exist between what was being taught in our schools and what employers actually looked for in prospective employees. A first review was headed by Brian Finn, then Chairman of IBM Australia. The work of the Finn Committee was then further refined in another review led by Eric Mayer, former Chief Executive of National Mutual.

In September 1992, a report defining the 'key competencies' which it was thought schools ought to deliver was handed down by the Mayer Committee. The report covered principles governing national assessment of competencies and steps recommended for achieving the implementation of their development in secondary schools.

A wide debate was triggered by the Mayer Report and, needless to say, some differences of views emerged in the education profession. However, the subsequent wide interest in the development of these competencies in schools reflects general acceptance of their value. In many ways, this acceptance and interest represents a major shift in the thinking and focus of educationalists in Australia.

Here I will simply focus on the seven competencies identified. Just what did this committee see as critical in competencies for young people starting their working lives?

The following table summarises the Mayer Committee's findings.

## Table 2.1 The Mayer Committee's key competencies

**Collecting and analysing and organising information**

The capacity to locate, sift and sort information in order to select what is required, present it in a useful way and evaluate both the information itself and the sources and methods used to obtain it.

**Communicating ideas and information**

The capacity to communicate effectively with others using the range of spoken, written, graphic and other non-verbal means of communication.

**Planning and organising activities**

The capacity to plan and organise one's own work activities, including making good use of time and resources, sorting out priorities and monitoring one's own performance.

**Working with others and in teams**

The capacity to interact effectively with other people, both on a one-to-one basis and in groups, including understanding and responding to the needs of a client and working effectively as a member of a team to achieve a shared goal.

**Using mathematical ideas and techniques**

The capacity to use mathematical ideas such as number and space, and techniques such as estimation and approximation, for practical purposes.

**Solving problems**

The capacity to apply problem-solving strategies in purposeful ways, both in situations where the problem and the desired solution are clearly evident and in situations requiring critical thinking and a creative approach to achieve an outcome.

> **Using technology**
> The capacity to apply technology, combining the physical and sensory skills needed to operate equipment with the understanding of scientific and technological principles needed to explore and adapt systems.

Three levels of performance were developed for each competency.

Clearly, underlying competencies are much broader than the ability to excel in a particular mathematics test or to master a foreign language. They are much broader than particular skills we might envy, too, in later working life, such as the ability to understand a balance sheet, the ability of a surgeon to use a lithotripter or even the ability of a journalist to write fluently.

Underlying competencies are *combinations* of aptitudes, values, preferences and talents that deliver effective performance or general ability. The work of the Mayer Committee is certainly powerful intelligence as applied to secondary and tertiary education and initial entry to work, but can we refine a particular set of competencies to develop and carry with us through the later phases of our working careers?

## The role of emotional intelligence

Competencies underlying independent capability in our work and careers are affected by *emotional intelligence*. This is a concept discussed in Daniel Goleman's fascinating book, *Emotional Intelligence*.[9]

Goleman develops a strong case for the defining significance of 'emotional intelligence' in the maturation and development of human beings. 'In a very real sense,' he argues, 'we have two minds, one that thinks and one that feels.'[10] He asserts that '...emotional aptitude is a *meta-ability*, determining how well we can use whatever other skills we have, including raw intellect'.[11]

There is no neat categorisation of emotional intelligence in the

---

[9] Daniel Goleman, *Emotional Intelligence*, Bloomsbury, London, 1995.
[10] Goleman, p. 8.
[11] *Ibid*, p. 36.

book, but a number of key aspects do emerge.[12] According to Goleman, emotional intelligence includes:

- self-control, that is, self-management, self-awareness, self-discipline and the ability to control impulse and delay gratification
- zeal, persistence and initiative, including the ability to motivate oneself and to persist in the face of frustrations
- the ability to regulate one's moods (and keep distress from swamping the ability to think) and to handle stress and anxiety
- the ability to empathise, actually hearing the feelings behind what is being said and seeing things from the perspective of others
- the ability to create teamwork, build consensus, effectively persuade and promote co-operation while avoiding conflict.

The first — the ability to control and manage impulse — is probably the most fundamental attribute in emotional intelligence. Goleman writes:

*Being able to put aside one's self-centred focus and impulses has social benefits: it opens the way to empathy, to real listening, to taking another person's perspective. Empathy … leads to caring, altruism and compassion. Seeing things from another's perspective breaks down biased stereotypes and so breeds tolerance and acceptance of differences.[13]*

In a sense, Goleman's book came as an enlightening synthesis of much of the thinking and experience of my 30-year career in human resource management. Recently, I have been integrating my practical experience with a great deal of material now available on the subject of competencies in the work environment.

## Competency models

Along with others, I had been building models of which competencies seemed ideal in key positions and then trying to identify those competencies in interviews, using behavioural event-interview techniques to probe for evidence of them.

---

[12] A more organised categorisation of the elements comprising emotional intelligence is to be found in Goleman's subsequent book, *Working with Emotional Intelligence.*

[13] Goleman, *Emotional Intelligence*, p. 285.

A behavioural-event interview is one where the interviewer discusses a major project which the interviewee has perhaps initiated or been involved in, and probes at each decision point exactly what the interv--iewee did. The focus is on how the person *behaved*: how they operated as each circumstance unfolded. When undertaken in a skilful fashion, these interviews can often throw light on underlying competencies.

Richard Boyatzis — whose book, *The Competent Manager: A Model for Successful Performance*, is a challenging read and has produced seminal research in this area. In a study of more than 2000 managers in 198, Boyatzis developed an aggregation of attributes and behaviours which he felt were displayed by successful managers.[14] He and subsequent writers in this area have identified what, at some times, seem a bewildering array of competencies including:

- leadership
- team building and team participation
- communication abilities
- initiative and proactivity
- analytic ability
- information seeking
- curiosity.

But Boyatzis' definitions of the term 'competency' are for the most part vague. They are *combinations* of attributes underlying successful professional performance and they are typically derived statistically from studies of many instances of effective and not so effective performance in real work situations.

An overview of research on underlying competencies suggests that you could wallpaper a room with definitions of competencies. This is not really surprising when one considers the remarkable range of attributes and dispositions in human personality: the many 'differing gifts' present among us, as the developers of the Myers Briggs personality profiling approach put it.[15]

---

[14] Richard Boyatzis, *The Competent Manager: A Model for Successful Performance*, John Wiley and Sons, New York, 1982.
[15] Isobel Briggs Myers and Peter B. Myers, *Gifts Differing*, Consulting Psychologists Press, Palo Alto, 1980.

Underlying competencies are much more fundamental to success at work than pure technical knowledge. Knowledge such as the skills of understanding accounting ratios, or the variety of sophisticated instruments used in managing investments, foreign exchange hedging and the like, or of writing complex computer programs, may be critical in some working roles. But for people with such technical skills to effectively combine and communicate with others, being part of effective teams and creating an organisational capability, much more than technical knowledge is required. The 'much more' is, of course, a set of competencies of the type I have been describing.

There is no easy 'list' which simplifies the task of isolating the critical competencies. Nor is there a simple testing mechanism and a method for establishing their 'level' in an individual or even detecting their presence. Competencies don't generally result in formal qualifications or certificates. Yet they are of critical importance for organisations — and for the independently capable individual!

## Looking for competencies below the water-line

Hay/McBer is a respected professional consultancy to large companies throughout the world. Building on the work of Boyatzis, McLelland[16] and others, the group has taken the trouble to define an impressive array of competencies and then to develop methods for building models of 'ideal' competency profiles for key organisational positions. In attempts to reach a rounded picture of current or prospective employees, the metaphor they suggest is that of an iceberg. The idea is to picture people as icebergs, with their technical skills and knowledge representing the part of the iceberg floating above the surface of an ocean, and with their underlying competencies representing the much larger part that lies below the surface.

The metaphor is useful in the sense that in interviews we often look for and talk about the technical attributes and skills of people and even

---

[16] David C. McLelland has been a professor of psychology at Harvard University. He is the author, inter alia of the paper 'Towards a theory of motive acquisition', *American Psychologist*, 1965, pp 20, 321-333. He is also understood to have developed the Behavioural Event interview technique.

reach a fine intellectual rapport with candidates without really probing for the underlying competencies, that is, the less visible but more fundamental aspects below the water-line. It is no wonder that many interviews don't result in the most suitable selection decisions.

To help you get a feel for the competency definitions used by consultants such as Hay/McBer, those developed in one important published work (covering, in this instance, a generic managerial profile,) are summarised below.

## Table 2.2 Competencies at work[17]

| | |
|---|---|
| 1 Impact and influence | 9 Information seeking |
| 2 Achievement orientation | 10 Team leadership |
| 3 Teamwork and co-operation | 11 Conceptual thinking |
| 4 Analytical thinking | 12 Other base requirements: |
| 5 Initiative |     organisational awareness |
| 6 Developing others |     relationship building, and |
| 7 Self-confidence |     expertise or specialised |
| 8 Directiveness/assertiveness |     knowledge in a professional field |

*Competence at Work: Models for Superior Performance,* by L. Spencer and S. Spencer, explores these competencies fully and develops them at various levels. They are derived from extensive studies of people at work and statistical correlation of observed behaviours and groups of behaviours.

If underlying competencies are fundamental to success, and as we can't all afford a professional consulting group to guide us in developing an appropriate set for our chosen or 'next career', what are we to do? How can we identify those which are 'core' competencies, or of fundamental significance? How can we build the right 'kit' in the business of being independently capable? And can we increase our level of competency in any particular area?

---

[17] L. Spencer and S. Spencer, *Competence at Work: Models for Superior Performance*, John Wiley & Sons, New York, 1993, p. 201.

Stephen Covey's *Seven Habits of Highly Effective People* can be translated into the context of competencies. Covey's 'competencies' may be summarised as follows:

- be proactive — have a personal vision
- begin with the end in mind — be goal focused
- put first things first — employ principles of personal management
- think win/win — employ principles of interpersonal leadership
- seek first to understand, then to be understood — employ principles of empathic communication
- synergise — employ principles of creative co-operation
- sharpen the saw — employ principles of balanced self-renewal.[18]

Does Covey's list comprise the whole answer? Is adopting a 'habit' the same as defining and building a competency? We address this question as we discuss the working careers of some real people in later chapters and we will return to it in the last chapter. Habits, or clear patterns of thinking and practice, are very much involved in building competencies.

## Five key competencies

*The Titanium Professional* proposes that there are five broad underlying competencies which underpin independent capability across most professional careers. They gather together the majority of the wider lists developed in the literature of business and professional development. They are largely built on emotional intelligence, as we now understand it. They are:

1  **self-control and self-management**

   the ability to control impulse, handle stress and anxiety, regulate one's moods or mental state and be self-motivated

2  **initiative/proactivity**

   an ongoing positive willingness to look for new opportunities and new approaches in any situation

---

[18] Stephen R. Covey, *The Seven Habits of Highly Effective People*, The Business Library, Melbourne, 1992.

**3    an ability to empathise**

to perceive the feelings of others and to understand the causes of
those feelings

**4    effectiveness with others**

moving through co-operativeness, to an ability to create teamwork, to
leadership in providing direction and resources

**5    analytical thinking**

the ability to assemble, dissemble, order and interpret data.

Clearly, the first four relate closely to Goleman's material. However,
collecting, organising and analysing data at increasingly sophisticated
levels is also a necessary competency in the world of work. This fifth
competency perhaps stems more from raw intelligence, or IQ.
Goleman himself reaches conclusions very similar to these in his
sequel, *Working with Emotional Intelligence*.[19] A brief discussion of his
approach (and my own) occurs in Appendix 1 at the end of this book.

Each of the five competencies listed sustains and supports the
others. People who are seen as intelligent, effective and independently
capable at work are usually using these core competencies in
combination.

## Detecting core competencies in interviews

If we have, or can develop these five core competencies, we effectively
provide a foundation for independent capability in virtually any
profession. Let us explore them a little and imagine that we are looking
for them in an interview with someone.

### Self-control and self-management

How do we determine if someone has 'self-control and self-
management' — the ability to control impulse, handle stress and
anxiety, regulate one's moods or mental state and be self-motivated?

An interviewer might ask questions about some of the major

---

[19] Daniel Goleman, *Working with Emotional Intelligence*, Bloomsbury, London, 1998, p. 260.

challenges and changes faced in the recent past. 'Tell me about some major challenges you have faced in your last position?' The interviewer would target particular incidents and issues and try to get a picture of how the person managed himself or herself. An attempt would be made to establish how the person thought, what kind of self-talk they used in the situation, how they responded to criticism and personal pressure, and how they created an environment in which they could operate effectively.

During difficult industrial negotiations, with pejoratives and personal abuse peppering the dialogue, I have seen people with a remarkable ability to think through issues and handle themselves with dignity in the most strained of situations. For all that we might bemoan the nature of politics, we sometimes see politicians handle incredibly confronting and provocative questions with calm and great self-control.

As a career transition consultant, working with displaced executives, much of my initial energy with individuals is spent assisting them to see how much of the future they, in fact, control and can determine. It is a process of reinforcing their own strengths in self-management, in seeing opportunities for marshalling of their talents and in researching new fields of work.

### Initiative and proactivity

In an interview — and in the broader process of observing and learning from others — how do we look for initiative and proactivity? We might find our answers come from questions such as Whose idea was it that you manage that project? or What did you do when faced with that problem? or Tell me about a new area of activity, or a new proposal you have put up and worked on in recent years?

Proactivity is a bit of a buzz-word currently. It embraces not only thinking of new ideas and pathways out of situations, but also the notion of taking a positive line in difficult situations. The books of Edward de Bono come clearly to mind: they are peppered with illustrations of people finding new pathways, sometimes unconventional solutions to seemingly intractable problems. Edward de Bono writes of the need for a new, creative intelligence termed 'lateral thinking', but much of what he discusses is about being positive and then thinking beyond conventional boundaries in addressing problems. The state of mind and self-assurance required for success seem as important as a high IQ (which helps as well).[20]

In addressing the application of technology, particularly information technology, in looking for new fields of work, and in being open to new types of employment contracts or even self-employment, initiative and proactivity comprise a critical competency for the business of building future careers.

I am constantly surprised by the new forms of work and new enterprises I encounter in my profession. Despite my earlier comment about new areas of attention in the secondary education sector, there are sometimes huge gaps between what we learn at schools and universities and what we then do in later life. This is particularly evident in the world of financial engineering, in the new businesses being created out of software needs and Internet applications, and in the new service enterprises addressing the needs of extremely busy organisations and individuals. It is people, strong in initiative and proactivity, who are capturing the opportunities all around us.

## Ability to empathise

Why is it important to be able to perceive and empathise with the feelings of others? How might this competency be discerned in other people?

Again, a good strategy is to not ask questions in the abstract (such as, How good are you at reading other people's feelings?), but to explore or observe actual events, using prompts and questions like:

- Tell me more about that project where you were installing a new information gathering system at work...
- What did your boss feel about the idea?
- Why did she have those views?
- How did you persuade her to support your idea?

---

[20] A selection of de Bono's books is supplied in the bibliography.

- What were the feelings of the others in the group?
- Did you encounter any resistance? What did you do?'
- Did you have someone you were working with who seemed reluctant?
- What do you suppose caused this? What did you do?

These questions are used to learn about the skills and behaviours of those who sense and can settle and influence the feelings and emotions of others. They should reveal the kind of intelligence that sees the critical importance of emotions and feelings in filtering and conditioning how people behave. Through using questions such as these, it should be possible to discover people who listen (really listen) and absorb more than just the words of those with whom they interact.

In the pressured, result-focused environments of many contemporary organisations and practices, it does sometimes seem as if people's feelings and emotions are not given much weight. However, the prevalence of these cultures can distract us from identifying individuals who appear gifted in influencing others, in reducing the stress of harried colleagues, and in building their self-esteem. Increasingly, organisations seeking to sustain themselves beyond the next major assignment or project will look for people who are effective in this way. Technical competence alone will be seen to be of limited value.

There have been times in my career, more than I care to admit, when in something of a stressed state I have behaved irrationally, perhaps being highly critical of others, or working far too hard and ignoring other signals and events around me. And there have also been times when a good friend or colleague has caused me to stop and reflect on why I am acting that way, why I am choosing to be stressed, with a quiet question or two: You currently seem awfully stressed — do you want to tell me about it? It isn't like you to be as angry about this sort of thing — why do you think you feel this way? The questions have been put to me in a private setting, with acknowledgment that while I remain a valued colleague, my behaviour might be letting me down.

There have been other times when the encouragement and

affirmation of another has 'lifted' me to take on some new challenge which otherwise I might not have attempted: 'When I see what you have done over there — I reckon you would be terrific taking on this new project.'

People who can respond to others this way — who always seem to be quietly connecting with the emotions and feelings of others — have this key empathic competency.

## Teamwork and leadership

Next we take a look at discerning effectiveness with others — co-operativeness, an ability to create a team or get one working together, and leadership.

Conventional wisdom and the writings of a great many people have taught us that leadership is highly situational. Some circumstances call for the leader who will be first out of the trenches, providing example and inspiration. Other situations call for a 'coach' rather than a 'captain' — someone who explores strategy with the group and empowers individuals with their own particular blend of talents to respond in the best way for the good of the group. The terms 'leading from the front' and 'leading from behind' describe these two different approaches well. It is important to know when each style is appropriate: and the context and the dynamics of the group are key clues. There is, of course, much more than this to leadership.

There are also skills required in being a valued member of a group, in seeing the differences in others and supporting both individuals and the group as a whole. Empathy and sensitivity to the emotions operating in individuals have already been touched on — here we are referring to the patterns of feelings and interests of groups and the cultures they evolve.

An example of this was provided for me by observation of a manager of an express freight business — a business with a small staff structure whose work was winning business and administering accounts and who utilised contractors acting as owner-drivers. The owner-drivers as a group were heavily unionised and inclined at times to use their collective power to extract concessions on fee structures and exclusivity in the coverage of particular suburbs. During the day, the drivers were out and about, taking instructions over two-way radios, but in the early morning they would assemble at loading docks to take on freight brought in overnight — and inevitably compare experiences, do some bonding with each other and sometimes reinforce among themselves the conditions which secured profitable returns to themselves.

The manager of this business, and other managers of similar companies, operated under a great deal of pressure, with external competition, pressure on costs and constantly changing customer requirements running alongside negotiating with union representatives and drivers. But there were individuals who kept calm, who remembered to spend the early portion of each day down at the loading docks building relationships with the drivers.

The manager in question explained that a key issue for him in measuring the effectiveness and viability of his operation was the achievement of at least a fair revenue base for each driver. When the earnings of one fell a little, he would assign a sales representative to the territory to build the customer base. More importantly, he would do this in the midst of industrial difficulties and negotiations. He never lost sight of the need to build and sustain the loyalty of the drivers, even when industrial action was threatened, or when margins were under pressure.

Team developers and leaders, in situations such as these, build and sustain co-operative cultures. They listen to and acknowledge individuals in the group, they provide guidance and resources and then move out of the way, and they embody the core values of the group. At a loading dock, this means being able to take criticism cheerfully and just occasionally to be the butt of collective humour (even as the manager is looked upon to provide overall direction).

There is another type of leadership to be considered — leadership of yourself. It is the confidence and assurance mature people have, and it manifests as quiet and purposeful work while others are perhaps caught up in group emotion over one issue or another. It is present when you can stand aside from your own ego in an argument, or see the possibility of a bigger picture when the media or group opinion is running a particular line on a community issue.

## Analytical thinking

The last broad competency entails analytical thinking: the ability to assemble, order and interpret data. It is a disposition to look into information and to call for more of it in a desire to fully understand the causes of events.

Sometimes people without this competency react to situations with the combination of a little surface information, and their own experience and biases. They react too quickly and perhaps intuitively. People with competency in analytical thinking pause, however, and look more deeply into situations and data before reacting and analysing its meaning.

In the world of finance, this entails analysing numbers in balance sheets, profit and loss statements and cash-flow summaries and then perhaps reconstructing financial data to provide ratios and new frameworks, such as 'economic value added'. In the world of investments, people with this competency look at company reports, and then beyond these — at industry data, and at national and global political and economic data and trends.

Effective human resource professionals seek to understand more than the particulars of a specific organisational need, such as the need for a better incentive compensation program. Those with this competency look at financial and operational strategies and measures of performance, at competitor practices and at wider intelligence and experience in other countries with particular compensation strategies and then at the readiness and cultural imperatives and constraints of their particular business.

Analytic competency is a willingness not only to look at the facts of the situation but to analyse meaning and relationships between data independently — perhaps looking beyond the immediate situation — before reaching a conclusion.

With the growth in knowledge, the rapidity of change and the speed of communication, ability in the collection and analysis of information is becoming an essential competency. This competency is not sufficient without the others discussed, but then without this one, the others seems less than sufficient as well.

The combination works well in a Chief Executive Officer who says: We should look at this more carefully… What are the real issues here and how have they produced this situation? It appears in a colleague who brings new insights and direction to a complex problem. And it is very evident in the individual we saw at the opening of this chapter — the person who moves without much perturbation through employment, self-employment, big and small organisations, always growing, always managing that balance between achievement at work and a family and recreation. That person is someone whose thoughtfulness can always be relied upon.

Some might argue that the five competencies defined here are idealistic — perhaps not tough enough for the stress-filled world of business. Is there a need for controlled aggression — for a bit of 'instilling fear' in one's kitbag of competencies? This is what some people at the top may seem to do.

### Are these five competencies 'enough'?

This isn't a book about how to kick heads in a bull pen. Controlled aggression might get a result in the short term (with *some* people in *some* contexts), but it isn't a part of being independently capable. People wedded to controlled aggression are just as dependent on particular organisations and contexts as those who choose to be oppressed within them.

Some time ago, a female colleague came to me saying that one of the clients of the firm to which I was consulting had been fairly persistent in asking her out and had even waited back at the end of a day to press an offer to drive her home. The same client had been persistent in approaching a few other female staff. While my colleague felt she could handle the situations, she was concerned at the confusion and distress he had created in one of the younger female staff — who was wondering whether her helpfulness had been misconstrued.

I began thinking about how I might approach this particular client.

My first thoughts were to counsel him to modify his behaviour, although no threats would be involved. I thought that simply speaking with him quietly would have the desired effect.

However, before charging in — as I might have in earlier years — I had the sense to review the situation with another colleague, and to rehearse how the problem client could best be handled. The advice I received was to take a different line altogether.

'Why don't we simply invest a little more time in teaching the younger female staff how to handle these approaches effectively, when they are unwelcome?' she said. 'These situations are always arising in this office — where numbers of clients come in and out and where men and women mix. Perhaps we simply need to cover some suggested responses which acknowledge the client, but gently yet effectively head these approaches off if they are unwelcome.'

My colleague was demonstrating several of the competencies I associate with independent capability. She was also setting out to build a small measure of independent capability in others with her constructive response.

Are there things we can do to build these competencies — particularly in the future environments of work? I believe there are, especially if we look around us and become our own mentors in the process.

## Summary

Chapter 2 discussed the importance of broad underlying competencies in achieving 'success' in most working careers — competencies that usually overshadow IQ or narrower, specific skills.

Five broad competencies associated with success in achieving durable, resilient, independent capability in work have been identified. These are fundamental and the foundation of many of the more specific competencies we read about. As a reminder, they are:

1  self-control and self-management
2  initiative/proactivity
3  ability to empathise
4  effectiveness with others
5  analytical thinking.

This basic framework will be explored as the book develops. Case studies are used to illustrate the practice of these competencies in independent career development. We will also look at the place of values — at the weight which should be given to honesty, ethical standards, principle-centred leadership — in being independently capable.

Chapter 3 focuses on strategies to become independent and capable in the future world of work, using these competencies as a foundation.

# *chapter three*

**Anticipating the future**

How can we operate successfully in the future world of work? There is not much point defining the perfect 'lone ranger' for a disappearing 'Wild West' scenario. Let us look at how we might operate in the organisational settings of the future, rather than ask how to operate effectively in the passing models of current organisations.

This chapter looks at six major influences on the nature of work as the twenty-first century commences:

- globalisation
- technology
- communications
- the changing expectations of workers
- changes in organisations
- the increasing velocity of change itself.

Many 'future studies' refer to the influences of globalisation, technology and communications. We will look at these influences separately, but their *convergence* lies at the heart of what is now commonly referred to as the 'knowledge economy'. This label distinguishes our present era from economic periods based on agriculture and on manufacturing. The drivers of modern Western economies are organisations that are building and assembling knowledge and information flow.

Undoubtedly, trends in globalisation, technology and communications will be key influences in what unfolds for organisations, and for the changing nature of work. These forces are also producing changes in the economies, political structures and cultures of countries, in markets and in the viability of businesses.

There are additional influences—some rather more subtle—with implications for the changing nature of work. A fourth influence is a shift in the expectations of the next generation of working adults. Noel Turnbull calls these people 'Generation MM' in his book *The Millennium Edge*. These are the first generation to take their place as employees and self-employed in the twenty-first century, and they think and feel about work very differently to their grandparents, or even their parents.[21]

---

[21] Noel Turnbull, *The Millennium Edge*, Allen & Unwin, Sydney, 1996.

I have touched already on changing practices in the construction and deconstruction of businesses, such as the trend of outsourcing various functions, but there are other trends in the ways that organisations structure themselves which the 'titanium professional' must grasp and assimilate. I have grouped these as a fifth influence on work.

Finally, there is the increasing velocity of change itself. The rapidity of change is producing its own repercussions in and beyond the workplace. We will consider how to 'travel' independently and capably in the stream of change itself.

Assimilating and anticipating forces such as these is crucial in sustaining independent capability. Our hypothetical role model will be appraising issues within and beyond work thoughtfully, rather than reacting too quickly to events in a narrow context. He or she will try new methods and new technologies as they present themselves. They will be alert to the feelings of others and especially sensitive to the differences in priorities and aspirations of the incoming generation at work. And finally, our titanium superhero will be reading and reflecting about all six forces of change, analysing the issues with patience and tenacity.

Let us now look closely at the six forces of change and their implications for those independent travellers.

## Globalisation

Businesses operate across country boundaries with increasing frequency. Businesses must now make investment decisions in the light of international markets, economic and regulatory environments, input costs and the like with scant regard to the economic impact these decisions will have on communities or upon individuals working for them. Globalisation means locating specialist suppliers in one country to service needs in many others. It means quickly assimilating design or process or technology improvements in one location and spreading the benefits of these across all locations.

## Dimensions of globalisation

Kenichi Ohmae sees the global economy as the conjunction of five forces:

- booming regional economies
- new media and information technology
- universal consumer values
- emerging global standards
- opportunities for corporate cost sharing.

In 'Life in the Round', Ohmae writes:

*Corporations and customers are able to move more freely in and out of countries. Services and information, spanning the planet, have supplanted manufacturing as the primary source of wealth and whatever the business or mission, the name of the game has become intelligence.*[22]

Thomas Friedman believes we need to look through at least six dimensions to make sense of globalisation. They are:

- politics
- culture
- technology
- finance
- national security
- ecology and environmentalism.

Friedman says:

*You cannot explain one without referring to the others and you cannot explain the whole without reference to them all.*[23]

In his very interesting book, *The Lexus and the Olive Tree,* Friedman discusses what he calls the 'democratisation of technology' through innovations in computerisation, telecommunications, miniaturisation, compression technology and digitisation. These processes have spread the practical applications and benefits of technology downwards and across whole populations rapidly.

---

[22] Kenichi Ohmae, 'Life in the Round.' in *Management Today*, September 1998, p. 8.
[23] Thomas Friedman, *The Lexus and the Olive Tree*, HarperCollins, London, 1999, p. 41 and *passim*.

Friedman discusses the 'democratisation of finance', through widespread access to securitised loans, bonds and shares, spreading access to investments and risks through widening groups in all major economies.

And he talks of the 'democratisation of information' through globalised television and the Internet.

The information revolution and these three 'democratisations' are said to have greatly lowered barriers to entry in any business and 'radically increased competition and the speed by which a product moved from being an innovation to being a commodity'.[24]

People setting out to be independent and capable need to be flexible and quick to see what we might learn in these contexts and not to be wedded to local traditions and practices. In particular, we must not rely on tenure, security, loyalty or continuity in our particular bit of the organisation — globalisation may see it closed down or relocated with very little notice at all.

Titanium professionals use an international outlook and the benefits of globalisation to find an independent place in the emerging world of work. Travelling widely, reading journals and books that transcend national perspectives, and continual curiosity about international events and trends overseas seem essential.

The subject of 'balance' will appear frequently as you read on. Here the message is that we need to balance daily operating pressures — the pressures to do many things concurrently (and *now*) — with the need to read about the future and be open to international trends and other cultures. This, in turn, requires a mix of those competencies we have talked about: the combination of self-control and self-management with initiative and analytic thinking.

Having a global perspective means reflecting on and assimilating international trends. Take a look at the books and articles of Kenichi Ohmae, a prolific and prescient Japanese authority on international trends and organisations. The early discussions of Naisbitt in his books

---

[24] *Ibid.*, pp. 17–18.

*Megatrends* and *Megatrends Asia*[25] are also absorbing — even though recent events may have overtaken some of his predictions! Subscribing to international magazines widens perspectives and builds awareness of the differences in thinking and values of different cultures.

The end of the twentieth century is a period of some volatility in the economies of Asia and Eastern Europe, with tensions between Western codes of practice in commerce and the unravelling of the more traditional 'favours and obligations' codes in some of the emerging economies.

Useful perspectives in reflecting on global issues and trends include:

- the fragmentation of Christian religious bodies and of Islam — with a concurrent rise in fundamentalist forms and religious influence in governments and commerce
- the final throes (one hopes) of repressive governments in Europe and in Eastern countries, and of the intermingling of corruption with commercial regulation
- a rise in 'planetism' and world governance, coincident with outbreaks of tribalism — eloquently explored in Peter Ellyard's *Ideas for a New Millennium*[26]
- an apparently opposing trend [in countries like Indonesia and Malaysia] towards a focus on nationalism and external adversaries in times of economic and political stress.

This is not the place to explore these developments. Independent capability increasingly requires however, an openness to and an ability to explore the implications of such global issues in international business relationships and in travel and assignments offshore.

## Balancing your sensitivity and your values

We need not necessarily compromise our values and principles while working in different cultures and with different organisations, but we certainly need to acknowledge and be tolerant of different values and priorities in the organisations of different countries.

---

[25] John Naisbitt, *Megatrends*, Macdonald & Co, Sydney, 1982; *Megatrends Asia*, Nicholas Brealey Publishing, London, 1995.
[26] Peter Ellyard, *Ideas for a New Millennium*, Melbourne University Press, Melbourne, 1998.

In the first of six years I spent working in Singapore, I inevitably made errors of style and judgment. I was nicknamed 'hard nose' by Singaporean union officials for my very Australian style of negotiation — it was a style singularly inappropriate for that part of Asia. Who knows what other pejorative terms were used before I gradually learnt some of the subtleties in the way Singaporeans interacted with each other? But the experience came at a critical time in my career and I learnt much from it.

Alf Clifton, a former colleague of mine, is the quintessential business 'operator'. He is an earthy Australian with a direct style, absolutely no pretensions, and some wonderful insights arising from his experiences acquiring and building businesses in a range of countries. 'Rules, regulations, laws, market conditions, accounting practices, attitudes and motivations all play a significant role in the establishment and success of a new business or acquisition in a foreign country,' says Alf, '…and woe betide anyone doing business in another country who does not do his or her homework in all these areas!'

Alf says:

> Business practices, conventions and ethics in France, Italy and Spain, for example, are quite different to those in Germany, the Netherlands or Belgium — and these things are different again in Poland, Hungary and Russia. In the case of the first group, considerable business is conducted and concluded over a long lunch, or a dinner, while in the second group rarely does one do business over either. In the third group dinner is the order of the day (for business transactions) and usually proceeds long into the night.

In many countries in Asia and perhaps especially in China, local business conventions are somewhat different from those in Western countries. Alf recalls his experiences guiding a joint venture in China involving Australian, local Chinese and Hong Kong-based Chinese partners:

> In the early days after signing the joint venture contract (within the first year of the contract) the chairman who was the signatory to the contract

was removed from his position. The incoming chairman would not accept the contract as negotiated and attempted to start negotiations again on certain points. His logic was that the contract was with the previous chairman and not with the company. The chairman under Chinese regulations (as they then were) is the company and as such is the legal representative. Accordingly, when a new chairman is appointed, existing contracts are null and void. It took some months to convince the new chairman that the contract was binding on the company and that he as chairman was a servant of the company.

The competency of empathy — being able to perceive and respond to the feelings of others — becomes critical as we struggle to see through the screens and filters of our own cultural upbringing.

Kenichi Ohmae provides a picture of the new globalised world of work in this comment:

*Leaders… [will] have to build networks rather than pyramids; learn to share, sort and synthesise information, rather than simply direct the work of others; rethink the basic approach to decision-making, risk-taking and organisational strategy; and create meaning and uphold values in flatter, more dispersed enterprises.*[27]

There are strong synergies here with the competencies we have been discussing. Clearly, if we haven't an ability to analyse, to create team-work across borders, to sense and understand the feelings of others in different cultures, to see and seize new opportunities at some times and to hold back at other times from our initial cultural responses, we will be limited in our effectiveness in the new globalised context. If this is the future world of work, then the competencies of independent capability become critical.

## Technology

Many writers about the future are fascinated by the increasing influence of technology. Changes in technology continue to change the nature of work. Aside from those directly employed in making robots

---

[27] Kenichi Ohmae, 'Life in the Round.' in *Management Today*, September 1998, p. 8.

and computers and the like, the changes are mostly in *how* work will be done rather than in *what* work will be required.

Biotechnology, laser technology, microelectronics and information technology are certainly having a significant impact on the way we work — with the last of these, information technology, probably having the widest impact.

Lawyers must learn to use information technology because of the speed with which it will facilitate researching case law and legislation. Doctors practising non-invasive surgery must learn new techniques and skills. Senior professionals in offices now use computers where formerly layers of analysts and middle managers provided the analysis and administration required.

Information technology change is also driving changes in the nature of work in banks, in transportation and logistics, in retailing and in fact most areas of commerce and public service.

Keyboarding, word-processing and basic computer operation are becoming threshold skills, taken for granted in almost all fields of professional work. Future mobility and growth will only come with an openness to the use of technology and some creativity in its application. Some people may shy away from technology and rest in the comfort of traditional methods, but while this is occurring, those with independent capability will doubtless be exercising initiative, proactivity and trying out an innovation or two.

The take-up and use of new technology — perhaps simply becoming computer literate — is as much a function of attitude and initiative as it is a function of particular aptitudes. The obverse of this competency is sometimes evident in quite senior people facing career changes and refusing to accept the possibility that the next 'job' might require basic computer literacy — word-processing and document creation. A personal assistant to take dictation simply might not be available next time.

## Communications

The most significant development of our time in communications is the Internet. With the emergence of the Internet, new occupations and businesses are being built around web-page design for businesses and the maintenance of information flows to these new 'shopfronts'.

Internet experts offer research services, marketing organisations and service providers are developing systems for penetrating new international markets and financial organisations are digesting the implications of the web for financial transactions and records.

The Internet and related intranets will revolutionise the work of banks, stockbrokers, retailers, libraries, teaching institutions, travel agencies and service providers, to name just a few examples.

E-commerce is obliterating geographic boundaries and driving the rapid internationalising of local and regional businesses. In the process new issues, such as those related to jurisdictions, are raised.

E-commerce is reducing transaction and information management costs in supply chains, transforming customer service and increasing the hours of operation of many businesses to 24 hours per day, seven days a week, with no geographic limitations.

According to Paul Twomey:

Greengrocer.com.au *has achieved the ultimate inventory reduction — to zero; nothing is purchased unless a buyer has already paid for it. Lower cycle times within Australian supermarkets have achieved savings of about $1 billion.*[28]

Jan Muysken, PricewaterhouseCoopers E-Business partner, says:

*With geography fast becoming history, a borderless marketplace is emerging where global suppliers, distributors, developers and customers converge on the desktop.*

*Recent surveys forecast that within the next five years up to 20 percent of business transactions will be carried out electronically.*[29]

And Dave Jacobsen, General Manager of Com Tech Online, remarks that:

*from the World Wide Web's inception, the Internet reached a critical mass of*

---

[28] Paul Twomey, 'E-liminating the deadweight.' in *Company Director*, July 1999, p. 14.
[29] Jan Muysken, 'Are your competitors just one click away from your customers?' in *Company Director*, July 1999, p. 25.

*50 million users worldwide in less than four years. This is more than three times faster than television and nearly nine times faster than radio.*[30]

We all need to become users of the Internet and open to the expanding possibilities of electronic information flows.

## Knowledge acquisition and the office of the future

Being independent and capable requires an aptitude for lifelong learning. Knowledge acquisition is a part of this, and being an active user of modern communications technology seems to be a critical skill in turn.

As Noel Turnbull says in *The Millennium Edge*:

*…knowledge acquisition…involves three skills: the capacity to research information; the capacity to critically evaluate that information; and the capacity to synthesise it.*[31]

Noel is talking perhaps more of cerebral intelligence of the IQ variety — but the parallel with proactivity and analytical thinking competencies is, of course, strong.

Some years ago now, a group of people within IBM constructed a picture of what work might look like in the year 2000. Their paper, called 'IBM 2000', drew up some scenarios to guide the focus of management development within the organisation.

These scenarios included pictures of young account managers pitching for the opportunity to install new hardware and software systems for external client organisations. In building their case (to win the business) the account managers were using an IBM intranet and sourcing intelligence from colleagues from all over the world who had undertaken similar work with similar customers elsewhere. The sourcing process was to occur — and clearly is already occurring — overnight, with electronic transmission of documents and dialogue across many continents.

---

[30] Dave Jacobsen, 'E-commerce: It's more than buying and selling online', in *Company Director*, July 1999, p. 49.
[31] Turnbull, p. 89.

The same young account managers were also going beyond IBM and using the Internet for wider intelligence. In the process, they were becoming more alert to the needs of the client organisations and their customers than the clients themselves!

'IBM 2000' was a thought-provoking synthesis of strategic thinking, reflections about service and people development, the internal influence of culture and anticipation of the creative use of technology. (I suspect there is a new version of this paper around now — looking at IBM in the year 2010.)

'IBM 2000' was one of the first discussions of the *knowledge economy*, a term not then in vogue. Increasingly, the rapid accumulation and management of knowledge within organisations and the application of knowledge-based services using technology, intelligence-gathering skills and collaborative cultures, will be a driver of success for both people and organisations. Skills in developing and applying knowledge across organisations are becoming just as critical as specialist expertise in more traditional fields.

Some pictures of the future show people 'at work' spending the bulk of their time at computer terminals, perhaps at home, working via electronic commerce. It is a world where the cut and thrust — and warmth — of normal human interaction has been displaced by information technology.

However, despite a strong need to be computer literate in the new world of work, this is not a valid picture for the next generation of professionals. There will always be a place and a need for face-to-face human exchange. People can only guide, influence and really respond to others in face-to-face dialogue. Emotional growth and emotional intelligence can only be nurtured in real exchanges with real people. For this reason, the complete transfer of large slices of work to home offices will not occur. However, 'hot desking' (sharing an office and desk with others in addition to working at home, in a client's premises or even from a car) is on the increase. Most organisations recognise the continuing value of people working with each other some of the time and in direct interaction with customers rather than with computer terminals.

## Information overload

Advances in the speed and utility of information technology raise another issue: the challenge of information overload. This is a real issue for many people at work. An article in the *Australian Financial Review* by Emma Connors began:

> *When Sydney lawyer Mr. Philip Argy returned to work last Monday after three months' leave, he found 13,619 e-mail messages waiting for him...*[32]

Increasingly, we need to find ways to identify and screen out information 'noise', and to focus on critical content. We need to learn the skills of skimming through papers and bulletins, mentally filtering out peripheral data, pursuing our own information objectives and carefully selecting information sources. Our time should be managed to reflect and assimilate information rather than to digest it partially and on the run in the busy 'doingness' of organisational life. As someone remarked recently: 'Don't just do something, sit there!'

Independence and capability require an aptitude for sitting, assimilating and absorbing before moving on — the skills of concentration and focus amidst information noise. This is a discipline which can be built in our lives, but it requires great effort at times.

## Changing expectations of the next generation

Another much less talked about, yet equally significant issue for the future of work is the changing expectations of young people, that is, our next generation of leaders, managers and professionals.

A good clue to these expectations appears in the writing of Richard David Hames and Geraldine Callanan in *Burying the 20th Century*:

> *People from all walks of life and young people in particular, are demanding a future that directs more attention to the human, spiritual dimensions of existence and less to the short term materialism and utilitarian attitudes. They are asking for a purpose that has the power to restore their faith in themselves and mankind.*[33]

---

[32] Emma Connors, 'E-mail a beast of burden to business.' in *Australian Financial Review*, Saturday, 25 July 1998, p. 4.
[32] Richard David Hames and Geraldine Callanan, *Burying the 20th Century*, Business & Professional Publishing, Sydney, 1997, pp. 239–41.

The aftermath of values and practices from the 1980s and the 1990s has led many young people to demand organisational cultures that embody openness, trust and dialogue. The next generation of professionals will simply stay away from places where downsizing and rationalisation have been endemic, or where bureaucratic practice and hierarchy are evident. These clearly are not places in which a measure of independence and individual capability can be achieved.

Young professionals already place a premium on being independent, on working smarter rather than harder, on caring for the environment, on creating a sense of community — especially within their own networks — and on working with ethical people whose practised (as opposed to espoused) values they can respect.

The values and practices of corporate life in the 1980s and 1990s are anathema to many young professionals today.

## Learning environments and appreciative systems

There is an emerging dissonance between the high pressure, frenetic, impersonal environments in many organisations (especially in central offices) and the more creative, 'human' environments sought by increasing numbers of thoughtful people. They are voting with their feet, as we'll discuss in the next chapter, and heading to smaller organisations or to self-employment. A steady dilution in the emotional and intellectual maturity of leadership in some organisations is the inevitable result.

Rejection of non-empathetic cultures is not confined to the next generation. For the most part, those retrenched and displaced in the current climate of rationalisation come to similar views. Increasingly, people will select more carefully their working environments. In turn, they then need to develop skills that support openness, dialogue, and organisational learning, since in many ways people create their own environments. An increasing number of books about creating 'soul' in the workplace and being 'calm' in the maelstrom of activity are being published and purchased — another 'industry' or professional service opportunity perhaps?

The competencies underpinning independent capability do require a little more than simply a set of attitudes, or a desire to be calm in the face of adversity.

Much has been written about creating 'learning organisations', perhaps in reaction to the chord this powerful phrase has struck in so many. It is also a reflection on the 'learning disabilities' prevalent in so many contemporary organisational cultures.

A learning culture is not something easily 'engineered', brought about through a training program or an inspirational seminar. Organisational cultures are as much a function of *practices* as of attitudes (or sentiments displayed on wall posters). The key practices here start with the example of those at the top. Learning organisations come into being when chief executives and their immediate colleagues are highly effective listeners skilled at dialogue rather than monologue. Learning organisations are created by leaders who are open to change and learning, who have humility and the wisdom to learn from everyone around them, and who encourage the open delivery of key information to all organisation members, building trust and collaboration in the process. (One of the tests of the 'learning ability' of an organisation is to review its response to mistakes.)

These are first and foremost individual talents — which by example tend to influence organisations. Just as we should select organisations carefully in the business of growing independent capability — ones where learning is fostered — so too we need to develop the skills outlined here in creating such an environment around ourselves.

Hames has a somewhat more elusive but thoughtful perspective on the mix of individual talents involved in creating a learning environment. He develops the notion of an 'appreciative system', referring to thinking holistically in a way that comprehends the values and standards now being sought by so many people.

*An appreciative system is a self-organising system able to 'learn' its way into preferred futures, in ethical reciprocity with its environment and in ways that are 'appreciative' of all stakeholders' needs, expectations and desires.*[34]

---

[34] Hames, p. xiv.

Independently capable people in the next generation of professionals will take a holistic, integrative view of work and of organisational decisions. This is a perspective singularly lacking in some organisations, who currently have a relatively narrow preoccupation with short-term shareholder returns in the corporate community.

Effective and attractive organisations of the future will be better at integrating the interests of staff, customers, communities and even nations in the stream of operating and strategic decisions. And staff within them will respond primarily to collaboration, empathy and individual acknowledgment — not to coercion. These elements will become implicit parts of the 'contract' sought by those who want a measure of independence within organisations.

Work is becoming different, coming out of the current decade or two of relentless pressure and the sublimation of many of these values. Part of being independently capable is absorbing and leading these changes.

Titanium professionals need to be in charge of themselves, rather than be swept along by mindless organisational pressure. They read and gather intelligence widely. They are more sensitive to the different and changing agendas and patterns of thinking of others. They are effective with others in the absence of formal hierarchy. And they have the ability to look at and analyse what is happening around them constantly. A positive picture of work in the future *requires* these competencies of independent capability.

## Changing trends within work

We have already explored the impact of the devolution of work to small, often separate, specialist providers. Some forms of 'old' work are becoming specialised or concentrated in niche service providers. And new 'work' is emerging to fill the many niches and cracks in formerly comprehensive organisations. Some new 'work' is the result of the convergence of new technologies as well.

### New work

New work is also emerging as a result of wider trends. These include the need to call for specialists to assist organisations in influencing their environments. New work entails providing services to relieve the stress and pressure among those who do more 'regular' work — and for those who cannot find work. New work includes servicing the growing need we all have to learn new skills, such as how to manage our own superannuation funds.

New work includes:

- designing, installing and modifying information systems
- crafting information system strategies to complement broader business objectives
- financial planning for individual investors
- managing intellectual property, especially in information systems and software companies.

Work is also created by changing regulations and legislation. A recent legislative change in my home state will spawn a new occupation inspecting and auditing the 'food safety management plans' of those who retail food.

It is anticipated that when current university students finish their studies, 30 to 40 percent of jobs available will not even have been in existence when they started tertiary study.[35] New enterprises are being built around these fields and some are led by highly independent and capable people.

## New approaches to work

Approaches to work have also changed. Within more enlightened organisations, new approaches include using temporary project teams and much flatter structures, and temporary alliances between organisations, raising a need for different skills and mind-sets in those who must build and manage such collaboration.

Robert Johansen and Rob Swigart talk of 'anytime/anyplace' work in the 'fishnet' structures of the future in *Upsizing the Individual in the*

---

[35] Simon Pristel, 'Training the key to future jobs.' in *Herald Sun*, 25 January 1997, p. 18. This is my summary of a comment by David Benn quoted in the article. Benn is the Managing Director of search and recruitment firm, Korn Ferry.

*Downsized Organisation.* The fishnet metaphor emphasises the lessening importance of traditional hierarchy and the growing importance of networking across boundaries and in many different directions to achieve organisational and personal outcomes. They also draw attention to an article by Larry Hirschorn and Thomas Gilmore about the four 'psychological boundaries' under siege in the emerging global business environment. These four boundaries are the:

- authority boundary (who is in charge of what?)
- task boundary (who does what?)
- political boundary (what is in it for us?)
- identity boundary (who is and isn't, one of us?).[36]

It is clear, and the authors of this article imply this, that boundaries (and perhaps clear accountabilities) are going to be needed. The concept of true 'boundarylessness' is an unrealistic one. Certainly one of the challenges for our independent traveller in this emerging world will be the one of managing 'Which hat am I wearing at this time?' In the absence of tight, centralised reporting protocols members of temporary project teams will need greater skill than previously required to sort out accountabilities, working arrangements and leadership sharing. Responsibility won't attach to positions in organisation charts (because there won't be any charts), but it will attach to those with independent capability.

When we read of the temporary project teams put together in modern software companies, hierarchy appears to be absent and teamwork and creativity given a premium. They sound like exciting places to be in! But we also read of burnout and high staff turnover on the completion of particular projects. Maybe there are other sides to these apparently attractive working notions. In all probability, people will continue to build careers around a particular core skill or profession, with periodic or parallel work in teams. Working careers will rarely, if ever, be simply sequences of participation in project teams alone.

---

[36] Larry Hirschorn and Thomas Gilmore, 'The new boundaries of the boundaryless company.' in *Harvard Business Review*, May/June, 1992, p. 104.

Having said this, more work in the future will be team based, with fudged lines of authority and with a need for informal, non-hierarchical leadership. Effectiveness with others and an ability to create teamwork with high sensitivity to the feelings of others are two of our foundation competencies, and we can see how essential they will become in the future.

The good news is that these trends are producing much more rounded people and much more interesting careers for those who set out to build the right experience. A more challenging implication of the trends is that new work usually requires high levels of initiative and proactivity. To succeed, people need to continuously assess who their customers, 'market' or clients are and what they want. How may value best be delivered?

These are some of the realities both within organisations and for those who are self-employed. The convergence of technology, communications systems, globalisation and the emergence of new fields of work provide challenges — but also opportunities — for those determined to carve an independent path.

## The impact of change

In our communities we are seeing change and its consequences all around us. The way we live, work and 'operate' seems to be constantly changing, sometimes for the better and sometimes not. The mix of competencies we develop, when becoming independently capable, is a good underpinning for being able to cope with and grow with change occurring around us.

For some, too much change is destructive. Richard David Hames puts it this way:

*Where once people had much greater certainty about their worth, position and role in society and were also definite about the personal contribution they could confidently expect to make, for many people there is now a sense of detachment and isolation from the mainstream. We no longer have a shared sense of purpose or direction.*[37]

---

[37] Hames, p. 241.

Reaction to too much change is evident in a retreat to more enclosing and 'secure' communities, in religious fundamentalism and in 'clear and meaningful' pursuit of single issue politics, where simple slogans provide comfort and certainty. The attraction of the international Greenpeace movement and of the ultra-right-wing political party spawned by Pauline Hanson in Australia, rests in part on the appeal of clearly defined causes in a complex and uncertain world.

As Noel Turnbull puts it:

*Change and uncertainty unsettle the vast majority of people. They become frightened and apprehensive. The more change the more fear and the more fear the more people become alienated and despairing. The greater the despair and alienation the greater the desire to develop a sense of belonging and security. Thus as the world becomes more global, the more important it becomes for individuals to define themselves in terms of place, family and community.*[38]

Turnbull discusses the 'gap' between the perspectives of those within organisations — dealing with one set of financial and working imperatives — and the perspectives of the customers and communities with whom they interact, who are looking for identity and security. If organisations don't see the disconnections between how they talk and think and the communities in which they will be operating, they run the risk of major mistakes in strategy.

But what about the impact of change in *individual* working lives — and what are the implications for attempts to be self-directing and effective within such contexts?

## Managing yourself

We need to be in charge of ourselves rather than being buffeted by change against our wills. We need to anticipate events and seize control of their consequences, as expressed in that wonderful quote by George Bernard Shaw in *Man and Superman*:

*This is the true joy in life, the being used for a purpose recognised by yourself as a mighty one: the being a force of nature instead of a feverish, selfish little*

---

[38] Turnbull, pp. 20–21.

*clod of ailments and grievances complaining that the world will not devote itself to making you happy.*[39]

The key phrase here is 'recognised by yourself'. This seems to be a characteristic of independent and capable people: judgment is made internally. There is no primary recourse to the opinions of others in steadily building meaning and purpose in their careers.

The consequences of poorly managed change and of organisations where there is a culture of dependency and disempowerment are quite clear in the work I do, and are especially visible in people who are the 'victims' of retrenchment. With the removal of the identity of their titles and of employer-granted security many feel temporarily lost. How long they remain 'victims' is very much a function of their sense of independent capability.

Work in future will require not only the creation of a collegial, learning environment, but also leadership at all levels in helping other people manage change.

There are inherent contradictions between downsizing and rationalisation on the one hand, and the need to build collaboration and teamwork in (remaining) staff on the other. When the present era of deconstruction is done, organisations will still tend to favour small rather than large operating units. These will only be effective with strong teamwork and flexibility in thinking. What will emerge from some of the appalling human resource practices of the 1990s will be a renewed focus on excellence in human resource management.

Being independent and capable in the twenty-first century will entail being aware of these influences and being proactive in anticipating how they will change opportunities in employment and self-employment.

Having considered the six forces that will significantly define the future of work, it would seem wise to build a career (or several careers) drawing from a variety of settings and relying on the value of eclectic

[39] This is taken from Charles Handy's book, *The Empty Raincoat*, Hutchinson, London, 1994, p. 266.

experience. A young law/commerce graduate today might envisage, for example, an initial period in a large law firm to provide general professional grounding, then a period in a consulting group working with a variety of client companies. He or she may plan a spell overseas, perhaps in London or Shanghai, working in international law. Once this is achieved, the path could lead to a small specialist practice; to a role as general counsel to an international firm; or even to direct involvement in one or several business ventures. Careers such as these are increasingly possible, but success rests upon the development of the competencies we have been exploring. Academic talent alone cannot meet the challenges involved.

Given the amount and speed of change, we ought not to adopt too narrow a definition of our professions, be they journalist, teacher, doctor or engineer. The influence of forces for change is such as to make yesterday's professional platform distinctly limited in the future world of work. And in the gaps between the traditional professions, new ones are emerging. The CEO of a health services group may have begun as a nurse, but moved through administrative, team leadership, finance and government roles on the path to such an appointment.

We certainly ought not to depend on one organisational environment for security.

## A case study in self-management

We finish with a case study: the story of one person whose career illustrates the value of self-managed shifts in roles and organisations.

Ian Greenshields is currently General Manager Corporate Affairs of a national food manufacturer and distributor. Until very recently, he was one of the working directors of a successful, large public affairs consultancy, which has some 120 staff. He spent his time helping client organisations fashion responses to issues, carefully manage communications programs and influence their environment. His work in the consultancy group included helping government departments realise a mandate to reduce private ownership of guns and achieve higher naturalisation rates (Australian citizenship) among migrant communities. Ian led other consultants in a range of projects running concurrently and contributed to business revenue growth as one of the senior members of the management team.

Ian began his career in Canberra, as a librarian-in-training. He moved into direct government employment in publications activities and from there into advisory work within the offices of government ministers. After developing significant skills in issues management and communications work, Ian took on a role managing public affairs for a multinational corporation based in Australia. After five years in this role, Ian managed a further change in career, moving to consultancy work. He has now decided to deepen his experience in investor relations and commercial issues management with the move back to a corporate role — but even with this move, he is anticipating returning to consulting, perhaps on a part-time basis, when he reaches his late 50s.

Ian has combined an interest in horse-riding together with his organisational talents in another direction — he supported the Australian equestrian team in the Seoul Olympics and the very successful event team in the Barcelona Olympics in a managerial capacity as 'Chef d'Equipe'.

Ian has a robust independence about him. His interests in horse-riding and motorcycling continue. With his wife he is now raising a young family. Ian has a well-developed curiosity about history and a fascination for the machinations of politics and influencing community opinion. He has high natural energy and a sharp sense of humour. His interests are not limited by the confines of his work. How did Ian learn what he has learnt in the course of this career?

> It was much more through observation than formal training... I also learnt by simply taking initiatives: risking criticism by making suggestions and occasionally setting out to push the boundaries of my job. But you learn a great deal in the early years by simply observing how effective people operate...

And what did Ian feel he had to learn in the early years?

> How to marshal facts to reach an outcome... [being able] to deliver the results of your work in a non-confrontational way... Influencing without

asserting… how to manage people, how to influence more senior people, how to encourage, educate and develop junior people, enrol them to the cause, generate enthusiasm.

We had not discussed the competencies underpinning independent capability at this time — but Ian's observations were all about learning how to develop and apply them:

[People entering new careers]… need to be able to be persuasive, to be able to put a view to senior staff, to be able to cause people to shift in their positions. If they are dogmatic or bombastic they won't get people to work with them and they will find it very difficult to persuade people. Nor will they be given the benefit of the doubt if they don't get something else right.

If they are young, they should look for a mentor. This is extremely important. They should not think they know everything, but continue to avail themselves of external courses as required. Today's environment is extremely competitive. Lots of people now have Masters degrees and soon PhDs will be just as common.

You need to be able to network in your profession as much as you can, because this is a key way to learn.

You need to be acquisitive with knowledge. Seek information which will give value for you.

Finally, on surviving and growing in the pressures of corporate life:

Set yourself milestone markers—and at each point of achievement and completion, ask yourself if this is what you want to do. Ask yourself if you are ready to commit to the next milestone.

Clearly define the area(s) in which you are competent. If you stray outside [these] and are wrong, you will be seen to be flawed. That perception can apply to all that you do.

In these situations, Ian questions whether you can risk too many mistakes:

Don't let the pressure-cooker situations become the reality you accept for the balance of your life. It can take courage to step back and do something different—but without it you can hardly describe yourself as independent.

Many of the things Ian refers to, in discussing his career and his career moves, reflect the exercise of underlying competencies rather than specific skills or IQ.

What Ian has said is interesting — but what he has done is just as interesting. In the course of his career, he has deliberately sought out different environments at key development points in his profession and triggered the changes. He has taken charge of his own moves, anticipating changes and moving to build opportunities. One of these was to combine an interest in broadening his career platform with his extensive experience in government relations and policy formation with the completion of a Masters degree in communications. He did this as a mature-age student while holding down a full-time senior managerial role.

Ian is quick to sense the feelings of others and to comprehend the issues influencing a group. He is a natural (and quiet) leader, and ready at most times to give pause for thought and a bit of analysis. In short, Ian seems to embody independent capability.

## Summary

In this chapter we have explored some of the changes that face us in our future professional lives. Those trends and their implications for independently capable people are summarised here.

- The increasing globalisation of communities and organisations makes it imperative that we assimilate global thinking and become more sensitive to the differences in thinking and acting in different cultures.
- We need to become *users* of new technology and remain open to the possibilities change will bring, rather than be frightened by it, or always in retreat.
- We also need to be open to, but in control of, the explosion of information now assailing us from new directions.
- We need to be sensitive to the values of the next generation of professionals and to create learning organisations around us, by the

practices we adopt, by listening and by encouraging collegiality. Hard, driving, autocratic environments are places where truly independent people pause only briefly, to learn what is there before moving on.

- There is 'new' work to be had out there, and we need to watch it emerging and see what opportunities it presents.
- The best way to manage change, and manage ourselves amidst change, is to hold to a path we are constructing for ourselves. We should strive to practise self-control and to reflect continuously on what is going on around us and what it means. The worst response is to become a victim—someone helpless and lost on whom change is imposed.

# *chapter four*

**Building independent capability within organisations**

For most of us, of course, work usually begins in an organisation. In an organisation we are employees, and as employees we do what we are told. We are not really given much opportunity to be independent and capable. At least, this *seems* to be the case.

However, conventional perspectives here need to be challenged. We can and we must be as independent as possible — certainly in the way we manage ourselves. So how do we set out to grow independent capability as an employee in someone else's organisation?

We also need to think about the changing realities of organisational life. There is not a great deal of value in talking about how to be independent and how best to maximise one's opportunities in the organisations of the past. Better that we learn to operate effectively in the very different organisational future that is unfolding.

Just what are organisations becoming? The causes of change and its effects have already been addressed. Now it is time to look at the implications for organisations.

## What are organisations becoming?

If the mass of literature about organisational trends and change is distilled, there are six realities about future organisational life to assimilate. These trends have been summarised in Table 4.1 to show where we are coming from and where we appear to be heading in organisational life. Inevitably, some organisations will remain influenced by past structures and cultures for some time to come and others will look like those of the future much sooner.

## Table 4.1 What is happening to organisations?

**Moving from:**

Organisations of the past have tended to be relatively stable, with fixed core disciplines, a steady range of products or services and a reasonably constant customer base.

**Becoming:**

Organisations are becoming more transient, less stable and more prone to restructuring and 'unbundling'. This trend will continue. The drivers of change are technology (including widening information flow), the shifting bases of competition (both locally and globally), chief executive mobility, and impatience in shareholders, and they will continue for decades.

**Moving from:**

Organisations have been hierarchical, with 'command and control' systems, well-defined roles and career paths, and formal training programs.

**Becoming:**

Organisations are becoming flatter, and less hierarchical. Professionals will work with loose and changing affiliations, in alliances rather than in hierarchical arrangements. People won't be taught and trained by bosses — they will be expected to attend much more to their own development.

**Moving from:**

There has been a constancy of size, or at least the notion that growing bigger was the broad aim. Great emphasis was placed on 'the team' and on the continuance and cohesiveness of the culture of the organisation.

**Becoming:**

This is the era of 'downsizing'. There is a huge contradiction between the obvious wisdom of building teamwork and learning environments on the one hand, and downsizing and outsourcing on the other. The contradiction may be resolved partially by the emergence of smaller, strategic business units. Enlightened managers may see that well-trained and focused staff, and the shared intellectual and cultural ability of the business unit, represent assets which should not be divested in an attack on current costs. These units may well be the more secure environments of the future.

**Moving from:**

In larger organisations, specialist departments have tended to look after the majority of the organisation's needs.

**Becoming:**

Smaller, specialised *businesses* will increasingly do the work of in-house specialist departments. Those who remain in the centre of the larger organisations will work longer hours than before. It is usually the case that people who work in small specialised supplier firms work pretty hard too!

**Moving from:**

In the not too distant past, loyalty to the organisation was celebrated and encouraged, with service recognition and some paternalism in looking after those who had been around a long time (even if they were not very effective).

**Becoming:**

The value of employees in organisations will increasingly rest not so much on years of experience, but on the dual skills of absorbing and using ever-changing technology and of learning, managing change, influencing and leading people who are independent rather than subordinate in any hierarchical sense. Those with whom employees must work effectively will include contractors as well as colleagues, people in other business units and those within the organisations of customers.

**Moving from:**

Work has been done in the office or at the plant, in a well-understood routine. Technical needs have been met by the technical experts in the organisation — the rate of change in technology has in the past 50 years or so been relatively modest compared with current rates of change in most fields.

**Becoming:**

Even within stable employment arrangements, the nature of work will change. Information technology is a pervasive influence — the growing trend is to work at home some of the time, using linked workstations. People share desks — or book an office/desk for time they spend in the workplace. People may work out of vehicles and at customers' premises with less opportunity to observe and learn from others and to learn in group contexts. Communication will increasingly be via the Internet or intranet.

To be independent and capable in the emerging organisations of the future, we need to understand and to work with these trends, not hang our hats on the realities of the past.

## How will change affect individuals in organisations?

We need to fashion the skills and abilities demanded by the organisations of the future (as outlined in Table 4.1) as we manage our development. These skills will include building alliances with others in (temporary) project teams and being a project manager with groups of people who may not report to us, but will be working with us. This is where an understanding and appreciation of the concept of interdependence is critical.

The ability to draw from an ever-widening array of contacts and provide an exchange of value in turn is becoming a critical ability for 'success'. Networking requires self-confidence and a healthy curiosity about the world and the experiences of others. People who are good at networking can deliver information and capture opportunities for themselves and their organisations more readily than those who are reclusive. Tools such as the Internet are vital in developing networks.

. An implied skill in much of this discussion is that of being in charge of ourselves, that is, not handing supervision of our career development to some other (impermanent) person or division. And this, of course, is what *The Titanium Professional* is all about.

Dependence on the culture and identity of the firm, dependence on care from more senior people and the sort of loyalties of those who once belonged to the firm's '25-year club' are not the attributes on which to build careers and self-development for the future! If we will increasingly work with others in non-hierarchical relationships, then certainly we can and should hold to the values of integrity and loyalty to others generally. But subordinate loyalty to the company probably won't serve as a particularly effective foundation for career development in the organisations of the future.

## How do we find the right organisations to work in?

Even as organisations are influenced by future trends, there will still be good and not-so-good organisations to work in. In the good ones, work will still be arranged through people working together, where a collegial environment exists, where everyone is valued and where collective learning and capability are fostered. In these organisations, people may be able to survive and grow professionally without really addressing the issues of building personal independence and capability. These talents may even be delivered in the training and development offered in such environments.

There will nevertheless remain many other organisations where people are treated as units of production and where little real dialogue and trust are evident. Despite the efforts of Peter Senge[40] and others, the emergence of 'learning organisations' does not seem to be overwhelming (in numbers) those where a 'command and control' culture create the usual impediments to individual contribution. Sometimes politics and individual patronage become even more intense in the rationalised hothouse environments of modern organisations.

Is every organisation like this? No, of course not! We have to select organisations — information gathering even while being interviewed. We can and must perform our own due diligence before joining any organisation. We may be able to do some research before even throwing our hat in the ring for a job. Information is also available in the selection process itself — especially if interviews are seen as an opportunity to ask questions. We should balance formal conversations with a request to have some informal ones as well, perhaps with prospective peers and/or key internal customers for our work. Selection criteria have to include tolerance and responses to mistakes within the organisation. At an interview, questions should include 'How will you assess my effectiveness?' and 'What have been some of the challenges you have had to face recently — and how were they handled?' In independent discussions with others in the firm — if you can create this opportunity — ask: 'What types of mistakes do people

[40] Peter Senge, *The Fifth Discipline*, Doubleday Books, New York, 1994.

sometimes make in this role?' and 'How do you handle these?' and 'How does the organisation respond when there are glitches in the quality of its products or services?' and 'How would you describe the culture in the organisation?'

A long time ago I worked in the mining industry in Broken Hill. In any mine, there is inevitably friendly tension between the geologists and the mining engineers. Typically, the geologists asserted that fresh ore bodies lay in one direction underground and the mining engineers asserted that the right direction was quite different. 'No, no, it runs this way over here!' With their seniority, the mining engineers would hold sway and a new drive would be started in 'their' direction. After a hundred yards or so, it would be discovered that this direction was wrong and that maybe the geologists were right! So a new, better start would be made.

The various false starts, the hundred-metre drives leading nowhere, were destined to become permanent features of the 'map' of the mine drawn for the benefit of future activities. And the tradition was that these false starts should be named after the mining engineers involved. So we had 'LeMesurier's Fault', 'Connor's Folly' and so on. These engineers were, in my time with the organisation, all the very senior managers of the organisation! This was the genesis of an early theory of mine: that the way to the top was to make spectacular mistakes and to get noticed.

Providing trials and errors are honestly made — and without intent to damage a customer or a colleague — some organisations can be entirely forgiving. The issue is how the consequences are handled. When a mistake affecting a customer is redressed and dealt with effectively, the consequence can sometimes be greater customer loyalty. Mistakes can be the initial trigger for demonstrations of great integrity in people and in organisations, where the response is: 'I would hate this to happen again — what can I and we learn from this?'

Organisations which respond this way are much better places to be in than those where fear and blame are more commonly talked about. The organisation that you are looking for should be committed to project-based learning, constructive peer review processes, even a focus on building independent capability in people. A small number of organisations — notably in the information technology areas — now equip their staff for self-employment ('for life after your period with us'). These far-sighted organisations are equipping their staff today for the realities of tomorrow, when the organisation may outsource functions or change in ways which make tenure impossible to promise.

A large Australian law firm now offers each intake of law graduates the possibility of commencing a partially-supported MBA program at the end of their third year with the organisation. This smart offer has dramatically reduced turnover at a critical time in the development of the value of staff and at the same time helped individual staff members broaden their skills for the wider world at some point in their futures. In Chapter 1, we saw that traditional performance appraisal systems and approaches to succession planning have been too 'top down' driven and encumbered by bureaucracy. Managers in organisations have tended to do things *to* people rather than *with* them, training has been designed without real appreciation of the capabilities needed for the future of those being trained and succession decisions have been driven by an element of nepotism or favouritism. The message is to look at what really happens in an organisation in terms of the opportunities it provides and not to rely on formal staff development processes and systems espoused.

Even for people lucky enough to find work in great organisations, independent capability will be a survival essential! Even where there is a commitment to individual development and succession planning, managing the development of your capabilities yourself is still a necessity.

If these are the realities unfolding and we have done our best to select the organisation to work with, how should we behave as employees?

## Building independent capability in the organisation

The early period in a new organisation, or in a new job, is a critical time when you need to grow and use the key competencies of the independently capable. This is a period of intense observation, trial and error. It is a time for quietly interviewing anyone and everyone in sight: Help me to understand why we are doing this?; Who are we doing this for?; How do they measure value in what we do?; What is likely to change in their needs over the next period? Then, moving further afield and talking to others: What is your job?; Who are your customers?; How do they see value in what you do?; Who are the competitors for this organisation's work?; What is our strategy?

After any length of time in a new role it becomes harder to ask naïve questions like these — it is expected that all of this is already understood. Being an information seeker, right from the outset, tends to set something of a pattern or set of expectations around you. Being an information seeker and being ready to take initiatives and manage one's own mistakes effectively — and carefully choosing environments where this can occur — are initial actions in building independent capability in an organisation.

Next come the skills of observation, analysis and self-questioning: What is it that these other roles achieve in this organisation?; If I am to develop a broader array of competencies, what is it that these more senior people do?; How are they measured for effectiveness?; What are the technical skills and underlying competencies they need?

There is an assumption here which is, of course, questionable. This is the notion that our aim is to become more senior in an organisation. Seniority, or certainly mastery of a profession, often equates to more independence in an organisation, which has influenced my approach here. However, we can be independently capable without rising to great heights, if this is our choice. In Chapters 7 and 8 we look at the working lives of people for whom organisational seniority has not been critical in their attainment of independent capability.

One of the curious features of many organisations is that the key accountabilities of the various critical positions are properly articulated only rarely. When this has occurred, sometimes the summaries are relatively confidential — they don't form part of disseminated materials within the organisation. Sometimes, too, what is written down provides a pretty thin explanation about what the job really requires. The challenge is to map the realities out for yourself — sometimes by asking straightforward questions. Certainly, most people find it flattering to be asked what they do and what difficulties they need to overcome. This is especially the case if the questions come at an appropriate time and are asked by a good listener. We can hardly sit down each of the key people from whom we want to learn and subject them to full interviews about their jobs! All of us are much too busy for that. The process is simply one of asking a question or two on those appropriate occasions.

The premise here is that we are 'in' the organisation in one role or another, but that we are seeking to expand our capabilities and grow in responsibility. People who achieve independent capability in their organisations tend to be acquisitive of knowledge and always ready to practise what others in more senior positions do — at the right time.

Take, for example, the role of a Finance Director. Perhaps in written form one responsibility for this role can be expressed as:

*To direct company-wide financial policy, information systems and data collection across the company.*

Not very meaningful or helpful? When a titanium professional digs deeper into such a role and asks questions, they might be able to convert an uninformative responsibility statement to something like this:

*Production of clear financial policies, understood by both accounting staff and line managers. Effective weekly, monthly and other periodic reports within the decentralised context of the organisation, making it possible for the CEO to understand what is happening in all the parts of the business. Accuracy and integrity in the data and compliance with accepted accounting standards. Maintenance of high professional standards in key accounting and financial appointments.*

This is a bit dry, I admit. But for someone in a less senior role, the effort to tease out what the work really amounts to does show something of the big picture of what might be their next role.

Another accountability might be expressed as:

*Manage the financial well-being of the organisation so as to preserve the value and potential of the organisation in financial terms.*

Dig beneath these words, and we might find the real measures of effectiveness would include:

- achieving high standing of the organisation in the investment community and among shareholders
- achieving high credit ratings
- maintaining capacity (in financial terms) to grow and achieve planned broad business strategy.

Then we might probe *how* people deliver these achievements. What knowledge is required? What skills are required? How might an outsider see effectiveness in this role going beyond stated duties or accountabilities?

Questions like these get to the nub of most senior roles and focus our energies on what key people must deliver. Without this effort, energy can be wasted simply trying to emulate what people look and sound like.

During some consulting work with a specialist public affairs group, part of my work was spent building up a clear picture of what key roles in the organisation should deliver. This would help the consultants in the organisation see more clearly those activities which would earn them higher standing and remuneration in the organisation. One of the senior consulting roles was that of Key Account Director, and one of the key accountabilities of people doing this job was to 'develop and maintain professional standards'.

Well, reading this in a bit of internal literature would hardly educate a less-senior consultant! By probing, I uncovered a clearer picture of the indicators of effectiveness:

*Clear articulation of the issues/objectives for each client, clear specification of the deliverable, with time frames, then on-time delivery of exactly what was specified, collection of fees due and finally satisfactory client feedback, as formally solicited, after the assignment. Satisfaction of the executive group as to creative input, intellectual rigour, effective selection of strategy and presentation quality.*

*Effective consulting skills, in the sense of listening, influencing, educating, defining the assignment services and client relationship and responding to the client at all times. Measurable principally through client feedback.*

If all *this* occurred, then professional standards in the firm and with clients would be maintained! Our language and notes as 'private investigators' would never be as formal as this — but this approach is necessary to build independent capabilities in organisations. Develop pictures of what effective practice is in your organisation, which can then inform your subsequent trial-and-error initiatives.

Those who successfully manage their own development typically set out to work operating at the level, or in the way, the more interesting positions operate. People who achieve this inevitably become valued and eventually assume such roles. Most importantly, they have achieved this independently: they have driven their own development. But first, of course, we have to understand what the interesting jobs are there to do!

Another dimension of my work with the same public relations firm was creating an environment in which less senior consultants might negotiate assignments and set development objectives for themselves. Even where this is not a part of the culture of an organisation, at least some measure of this is usually possible.

## Developing independent capability in informal organisations

Even if the (increasingly smaller) business units of large organisations are great places to work, movement between them will be difficult. In the words of John Micklethwait and Adrian Wooldridge:

*Even in a big company, people can no longer afford to see career as a ladder leading straight from the humblest office to the boardroom. Rather it has become a series of islands connected by causeways, loosely governed by a small floating flagship.*[41]

In *Upsizing the Individual in the Downsized Organisation*, Johansen

---

[41] John Micklethwait and Adrian Wooldridge, *The Witch Doctors,* Heinemann, London, 1966, p. 225.

and Swigart talk of fishnet organisations. People in these organisations run the serious risk of being at times without contact or context, a consequence of the rising phenomenon of temporary teams and constant disaggregation of structures.

Johansen and Swigart also talk of 'anytime/anyplace' organisations, where 'job security will depend on being prepared for the next team assignment when the call is sent out'.[42] Downsized and delayered organisations run the risk of losing continuity where each must 'continuously scramble to recreate and maintain a sense of where they are in the marketplace'.[43]

It is clearly difficult to be effective in organisations of this character. In fact, in extreme situations, working in them requires exceptional resilience.

*Without continuity, a company becomes lost, unsure of what it is. If everyone working for a corporation forgot each morning the history of the organisation, where it started and how far it has come, along with its procedures and its web of relationships with customers, suppliers, competitors, vendors and among internal departments, the company would no longer exist. It would evaporate in institutional amnesia.*[44]

There is plenty of evidence around us of the re-invention of past skills and procedures in many recently rationalised organisations. If, at times, organisations around us are fragmenting, we need to create our own context and direction.

*Continuity is the product of the ability, culture, composite needs, desires, attitudes and experiences of the people who make up the organisation. In the interlinked complexity of the emerging global business culture, we all need a sense of balance and of being centred. For individuals, continuity requires a balance among work, home, leisure and community and between one's self and one's view of reality. By introducing new options, the anytime/anyplace office creates a sense of imbalance.*[45]

---

[42] Johansen and Swigart, p. 120.
[43] *Ibid*, p. 86.
[44] Johansen and Swigart, p. 87.
[45] *Ibid*, p. 146.

The titanium professional will have a portfolio of new skills helping them to operate effectively in such an environment. These will certainly include being balanced and also being flexible. But most importantly, this professional will need the ability to analyse and understand what makes the organisation and its customers tick, even when that organisation does not communicate its continuity and context very effectively.

In developing professional independence, we must look at what is *needed* (in the organisation and for its customers) as much as what is being *done*, and then build capabilities aligned with the organisation's necessary development. Successful, independent people look well beyond the narrow prescriptions of their roles and titles at the much bigger picture within and beyond their organisations and retain that perspective in their suggestions.

The capability development process is an active one. Independently capable people manage their learning through doing things — getting involved in projects, taking initiatives, making mistakes and learning from them, negotiating exposures and assignments which develop their abilities. The only person you have to negotiate with is yourself. Do I have the ability to do this? Should I give it a try?

Independent self-developers manage their own experience and they observe themselves in the process, as well as constantly seeking advice. They then move on with the new capabilities they have now demonstrated to themselves they have.

Many jobs or assigned positions don't properly address what the organisation needs. Despite all the rationalisations of the past, the stripping down of organisations and the outsourcing of functions, people have a remarkable talent of defining what is to be done in terms of what they feel most like doing!

One human resource professional recently boasted of his activity in launching 360-degree surveys in his organisation. These are quite stretching instruments which draw assessments of individual managers' performances from peers, from those above them and those below them in the organisation. It is a process that has captured the interest of a great many human resources people and their Chief Executive

Officers (CEOs). However, in the case of this organisation, much more fundamental issues needed attention. Poor levels of openness at the top (and no commitment to the survey process from the top), a hierarchical structure and diminishing confidence in the ability of the organisation to retain market share, meant that any 360-degree survey would be highly likely to be torpedoed or sidelined. It seemed likely to become another failed initiative of an enthusiastic, if immature, HR department. There were other things needed beforehand.

As another obvious example, many people have had the experience of working for managers obsessed with costs and restructuring to the almost total exclusion of a focus on customers and evolving market opportunities.

We need the ability to stand back and appraise the organisation and its context. Organisations in one form or another are the 'engines' of much of the economy. We need to keep learning about organisational life — without necessarily being seduced by one blockbuster book after another, each telling us how to 're-engineer' our company or 'compete for the future'. Management theory needs to be assimilated by aggregating a variety of perspectives, not slavishly adopting those of any one author alone.

How do we build 'intelligence' about the effectiveness of our organisation? Concern about looking to one management theorist notwithstanding, a great deal of wisdom over the years has come from Peter Drucker — a sort of constancy of insight amidst a great deal of noise and hype from other sources. One of Drucker's articles proposes that most businesses operate with an implied 'theory' (or paradigm) of business.[46] He provides as good a framework as any for us to better understand our own organisations. Drucker suggests that the paradigm — or operating 'picture' of the business — has three parts:

- **assumptions about the environment of the organisation, that is, society and its structure, the market, the customer and technology**
- **assumptions about the specific mission of the organisation**

[46] Peter Drucker, 'The Theory of Business.' in *Harvard Business Review*, September 1994, p. 95.

- **assumptions about the core capabilities needed to accomplish the organisation's mission.**[47]

If these assumptions fit reality and if they fit one another, the organisation is well placed to operate effectively. Leading organisations must test these assumptions continually and act where changes in practices and priorities emerge from the process.

The business plans developed annually in most organisations are largely a summary of the assumptions being made for the upcoming year and their translation into financial projections. Business plans have a habit, however, of leaping a little too quickly into brave financial projections — with more elementary assumptions being swept aside in the rush to produce impressive growth charts. It takes a brave person to ask of a senior manager: How exactly is it intended to achieve the growth implied in that chart? or We did not achieve that rate of growth this year so what will we be doing differently next year?

Effective people in organisations — those with a degree of independence in the path they carve — constantly test and explore all the underlying assumptions, not confining themselves to those which relate to their function. Their insights and leadership in questioning and responding to each of the areas of organisational life we've discussed are what gives them stature and independence in the first place. It is important to learn about the purpose and strategies of the organisation, and then focus on its environment, competitors and changing customer needs. Finally, question strategies and tactics. By doing this, we contribute to effective work in the organisation and we will certainly be learning at the same time.

It is concerning to note the lack of focus on customers in many individuals when reviewing their recent careers. Every organisation needs customers (to state the blindingly obvious), but sometimes we forget that it is they and their changing needs that provide us with a

---

[47] Drucker's explanation of core capabilities states that each has four elements: 'Those elements are *knowledge and skills, managerial systems* — tailored incentive systems, in-house educational programs or methodologies that embody procedural knowledge, *physical systems* including information systems and *values* — the attitudes, behaviours and norms that dominate in a corporation.'

set of income-earning activities (our job, business or role). Perhaps we need to step back more often than we do and ask some basic questions afresh:

- In my new career, who, exactly, will be my customers and what solutions do they need?
- How will they measure my effectiveness?
- How might I be perceived by them?
- How might I be perceived as being different (and better) than my competitors?
- How are their needs changing and what opportunities do these changes present?

Conventional wisdom has it that even internal departments, such as accounts and human resource departments have customers as well. But the same basic questions are all too often ignored. This becomes most evident when people with long careers in large corporations contemplate self-employment. For many years, customers and expected organisational remedies have been signalled to them. When embarking on a new career in self-employment, the fundamental questions about their real customers can initially be challenging. Sometimes the demise of careers and of whole sections of companies is triggered by the realisation that the services and activities being performed are simply not in line with the needs of external (or internal) customers.

Independently capable people ask the hard and thoughtful questions, sometimes covertly in their own thinking about an organisation and sometimes overtly, in the appropriate contexts. Asking thoughtful questions is often a much more effective way to demonstrate intelligence than making assertions.

## The penalties of corporate life

Much has been written about the penalties of corporate life — about the pressures, the inability to be in control of one's own time and priorities, about the politics and the stress caused by this form of work.

Organisations differ widely in their cultures and technologies and in the influence of people in senior roles. However, there is no escaping the realities of the pressures in many organisations. Partners in legal firms can be caught in situations where competition between them to generate revenue becomes inescapable. Line managers heading major divisions often face enormously complex and competing demands in achieving business growth, short-term profitability and the arbitrary demands of 'acceptable returns to shareholders'. People at all levels and in many functions can experience great pressure and debilitating stress. The notion of being in charge of ourselves, our time and our 'balance' seems increasingly difficult to achieve in the organisational context.

There are plenty of environments where the pressure to conform is high and where the culture demands extremely long hours, being 'with the team' in hard work, tough language and hard 'play' as well. Sometimes exceptionally strong leaders move into organisations imposing new disciplines and tough standards, cleaning out under-performing business units, demonstrating exceptional talent in capturing business opportunities and in attracting shareholder investment. These can be demanding people to work with. We either conform, echo similar sentiments and work like crazy, or we don't last long in such environments.

Is it feasible to be independent and capable in these environments — or must we 'hunt with the pack' and hope to keep up?

This is a multiple response question! At different times in our lives, we will have different responses.

There is no doubt that at some times in a self-managed career, a great deal can be learned in these environments. If some balance is achieved — managing time for personal relationships, for 'decompressing' and reflection — working with tough leaders, of the type described, can be terrific. The key is to see these periods in exactly this light: periods in which to learn. Don't become captive to this working style for a whole career!

There are plenty of people who *are* captive to such working lifestyles — and in no substantive sense are they independent. Despite material success, such people are often driven, unhappy with themselves, in less than full relationships with others and prone to allow their organisations and their title to define their identity.

When consulting, I continually come across casualties of what a friend terms 'the hurry sickness'. People in, or recently from, these kinds of organisations tend to speak quickly, exhibit tension and impatience, have short concentration spans and rarely show themselves to be good listeners. Over long periods of time, the real and alarming medical and social effects of stress will show themselves.

Survival in these environments depends on keeping intact an inner dialogue with ourselves to observe and manage the consequences. This means keeping in place an ability to ask ourselves: Am I going to allow this situation to stress me utterly, or can I step a little back as I do the work? Stress, even in the face of unreasonable demands and unreasonable people remains a matter of choice. The fact is, we *choose* to be stressed and we can choose equally not to be stressed if we have sufficient confidence in ourselves and in our integrity. A major test of independent capability lies right here: people who have achieved this condition simply don't allow unreasonable people or situations to create self-doubt or personal stress.

We may also have to become good at compartmentalising the different tasks and issues involved in high pressure organisational contexts. (I wish I had this skill!) People good at maintaining their own equilibrium in pressured situations seem especially able to place difficult projects or parts of projects into 'boxes', which they draw across one at a time and give their full attention without being distracted by the other 'boxes' nearby. They can focus intensely, concentrating on and analysing each issue as far as possible in the time they can give it. In the same manner, an hour grabbed here or there can even be totally dedicated to exercise, relaxation — even meditation — before the next task is taken on. For these people, weekends are often non-negotiable spaces for family and recovery. There is a wholeness about them which the unnatural pressures and demands of work seem not to touch.

Those who survive in high pressure situations are usually also good at maintaining a sense of humour.

If we can do these things and concurrently take some measure of control over our learning and development, we won't be psychologically as dependent on others in the organisation. We will be less stressed by the politics or power-plays of others, should they exist. Being less dependent on others for one's future, even within an organisation, carries with it a very real sense of independence, creating a barrier to some of the vicissitudes of corporate existence.

Independently capable people see themselves in a holistic sense, as a person, a loving partner or as a parent perhaps, as a son or daughter, and then perhaps as a doctor, or sales manager, or whatever other title applies. The organisational role is not *all* that they are. Those who are *not* independent and capable allow the organisation and their title to define their identity. They see their sense of well-being, self-esteem and security as being tied to the approval and direction of others in their organisational setting.

This chapter has been about being in charge of your self-development and being more than a little calculating and purposeful in negotiating your experience and professional growth. This can be achieved while in — and contributing to — an organisation, but at the same time not becoming captive to a quite unrealistic lifestyle.

Motivational speakers for decades have been teaching simple truths wrapped in the language of hyperbole. One of these truths is that if we act 'as if' we have particular talents and aptitudes, we will surely acquire them. If we believe in our diplomacy, in our ability to control ourselves in stressful times, or in our negotiating abilities, then visualising ourselves being successful in these ways and practising these talents will deliver them to us absolutely. I have never been too sure about the 'absoluteness' guaranteed by the self-visualisers — but I do agree with the thrust of this approach.

Most of the independently capable people I have known do believe in themselves and in their ability to learn whatever skills are needed for their working lives. A strong measure of self-confidence and the reinforcement of this in the internal conversation each has with themselves from time to time seems to be fundamental to their independence. It sustains them in pressured, political situations and permits them to move on.

Organisations can be stereotyped as places where politics and pressures prevent the full development of individual talents — but for independently capable people, they are simply environments for learning in a rather particular way and for a defined time only.

There is another response to the issue of political, pressured organisational cultures. It seems to me that this model or conception of organisational life is reaching the point of implosion. Within the next decade perhaps, new entrants to professional life will vote with their feet to remove themselves from these contexts, or not to enter them. People who avoid these environments are already electing quite different organisations and working arrangements for themselves. Many move to self-employment in a determination to create their own more constructive environment. Those who remain in pressured and political environments will become condemned to a life of following nervously, or with an aggression which is merely another manifestation of the fear of being left behind. But increasing numbers will work out new solutions. Unaware organisations will find that the real talent they need works elsewhere and has become inaccessible. They will also find that a culture of pressure, busy-ness, aggression and control is not, in fact, very effective in delivering quality work for customers.

## Summary

Chapter 4 has revealed some key ideas about achieving independent capability within organisations, summarised here.

- We need to take a long hard look at emerging realities for organisational life and equip ourselves for the future, not for the past.
- To the extent we can, we should select the organisation we will work with carefully — looking to what really happens among people in the area we are entering rather than what is espoused in staff development.
- We should adopt a questioning approach right from the start and define ourselves as someone who can be relied upon to ask interesting and thought-provoking questions.
- We should apply these skills to determine the nature of the 'real' work: why key jobs exist and how they are measured for effectiveness. We will recognise that what is needed in the organisation and what jobs comprise

may be different things. We should negotiate and create the *experience* which will develop the capabilities really needed.

- We should look around and at the organisation, using the frameworks of management theory. We need to build our intelligence about the environment, the customers, the mission and the critical capabilities needed in the organisation continually. We need the courage to ask basic questions about assumptions, all the time.
- We should adopt the state of mind and the practices of someone who is independently developing their own capabilities. In doing this, we will be creating (substantially) the very outcomes we seek.
- We should be independent as individuals as we move through organisations. We will avoid dependence on the culture, the patronage or the politics of the organisation for survival. We will not build our sense of self around these things, or around our work titles.

# *chapter five*

## Case studies in organisational careers

This chapter explores the professional experiences of two people who have achieved independent capabilities within organisations, Frank Whitford and Susan Holmes.

## Introducing Frank Whitford and Susan Holmes

Frank Whitford was until recently Managing Director of clothing manufacturer and distributor, the Sportsgirl Sportscraft Group. Frank was also a ten percent shareholder, following the buyout of the group by him and an international retail group at a time when the organisation faced liquidation. Recently, Frank proposed a management buyout of the business to the principal shareholder. The offer was declined and in the circumstances Frank offered his resignation.* He is currently contemplating a next career.

Frank began his working life as a police officer. He subsequently entered employment with the Waltons retail group and then, within that environment, moved into human resource management. Frank was next employed by Kodak, where he continued to develop his human resource management career. After 14 years he moved to the Coles Myer group, a much larger and more diverse collection of retail businesses, shifting his professional focus to a succession of increasingly senior line management roles. He reached the position of Group General Manager Retail Operations after eight years with Coles Myer, with responsibilities for $3.4 billion in sales annually, 25,000 staff and 72 stores Australia-wide.

Frank resigned from this role in one of a series of reorganisations in Coles Myer, but emerged as Managing Director in Sportsgirl Sportscraft and very soon thereafter became a shareholder in the restructuring of this organisation. It was a move to a more autonomous role in a much smaller organisation. Sportsgirl Sportscraft has around A$200 million in revenues annually and manages, or distributes through some 200 outlets in Australia, with joint venture distribution arrangements now opening in South-East Asia.

Frank is a quiet, very controlled individual with an air of

---

* Please note that since the text of this book was written the circumstances of this company have changed. See the acknowledgements for further information.

determination, directed not so much at the trappings of success but for
the success of the enterprise which he manages. He has been described
as 'a tough operator, who is extremely hardworking, has a precise
mind, is very strong on strategic issues, is capable of assimilating broad
facts and developing plans, is able to measure performance, surrounds
himself with talented people, works extremely well under pressure, has
good marketing skills and stays close to the customer'.

Frank is also described by a senior colleague as a strong teacher and
learner. 'He teaches his staff with great patience, helping them to new
levels of ability, but at the same time he is also learning continuously.'

Frank is the most senior of the case studies in this book — he was a
CEO and while getting to this level is not the particular focus of this
book, Frank is an unusual person in such a role.

Susan Holmes was until recently Executive General Manager —
Member Services, of the Royal Automobile Club of Victoria (RACV).
She was one of four general managers reporting to the Chief Executive
of the organisation and shared responsibility for the broad strategy of the
organisation. She had specific responsibility for a range of business units.
These included emergency road services, public affairs, publications,
three clubs and a major project involving the development of a new
state-of-the-art satellite-linked roadside assistance program. She oversaw
700 staff and a budget of around $120 million.

Susan's career has spanned physical education teaching, consulting
psychology, management consultancy, senior public service roles —
including leadership of business, consumer affairs and senior executive
policy and appointments, Chief Executive of the Small Business
Development Corporation and of Melbourne City Marketing, a
company established to regenerate the heart of Melbourne. Most
recently, she was in a line management role in a service organisation.

Susan is fiercely ambitious but, again, not in any material sense. Her
ambition is more for her organisation. She has a great determination that
the people around her should perform well and be developed. Perhaps a
little of her drive derives from her gender — her enthusiasm to prove to
herself and others that she is more than the equal of typically male

appointees in equivalent positions. She is articulate, passionate, energetic and hardworking. And she is pleased with the diversity of her career transitions. She is already planning where her next move may take her.

## How did Frank and Susan become titanium professionals?

How did Frank and Susan learn or develop the talents and abilities associated with being independently capable? Here we take a look at some of the factors they identify.

### Early influences

Both Frank and Susan watched and learnt from the example of others around them in their early careers.

Frank felt an early mentor had been Alan Jeans. Jeans has had an outstanding career as a football coach — the only coach to take Australian Rules football team St Kilda to a premiership. But in his early career, Jeans had been a policeman, for a time supervising a much younger Frank Whitford.

In describing Alan Jeans, Frank remarked:

> I admired the way he conducted himself every day: his deep thinking, his considered approach to a number of issues: his even-handedness, if you like. Instead of taking the everyday line of thinking, he tended to try and think about things differently, using 'what if' scenarios. He would often say: 'That is one point of view…'

Frank also discussed another great influence on his approach to work:

> I went from the police force to work in retail and I worked in the very early days at Waltons. There was a gentleman there by the name of Colin Grant and Colin had, I thought, a marvellous recollection of what he'd asked you to do. He'd ask you to do things and then some months, or weeks later, he'd come back and he'd say 'When are you likely to have that completed by? I used to give him an answer that was obviously always a little bit more ambitious than my ability to implement. Literally three or four days (and it took me many, many months to wake up to this fact) after I'd promised a delivery date, he'd come back to me and ask me had I done so-and-so.

I was always amazed how the hell he'd remembered all these undertakings so I asked him about this one day. 'Colin,' I said, 'I'm most impressed, this is now about the seventh or eighth time (and I didn't report directly to him) you and I have talked about something and I've picked up a pattern that within three or four days of the date agreed you come back and ask me if it is done.' I said, 'You actually don't go and check yourself, you come straight to me.'

And he said, 'Come with me, lad,' and he took me to his office, where he had a filing system. I don't think I'd ever seen somebody before jot things down in a diary and then commit this to a filing system. He had a marvellous methodology for actually keeping control of his business and keeping control of what was going on around him. There weren't just notes in there in relation to me, but to all of the key executives and this was time-dated and prioritised. So there were the two issues that were important to him — time and how critical the matter was. If an issue was critical then it had to be done on the day; if it was less critical then it took a lesser priority.

He taught me all about control and discipline and also prioritising. He really helped you think through priorities.

His management style was absolutely wonderful, I mean you never felt under threat, you never felt under pressure, in fact in the end you wanted to please the guy. You made sure you got the task done. This was 30-odd years ago and he impressed on me the fact that you had to wear a suit coat on the selling floor and a tie and your shoes had to be polished and so on. It was a very disciplined approach to business, which it tends not to be today.

But what I found in that environment was that you owned the work, despite the fact that he was very clear and concise about what it was he wanted you to do, you actually felt some ownership of it because he gave you ownership over time completion. And so you walked away with a clear feeling that it was your job, your task and not something someone else had given you.

So the important things I learned here, from his example, were to give people ownership of the work and yet to be disciplined in the way you followed up their commitment. Incidentally, he was consistent with all the executives — it wasn't just something he did with me. He had a whole process that he managed the company by.

What did Frank have to say on how this particular mentor handled things if you did *not* deliver?

It was very interesting. He would just reset the date with you. In the early stages, when I didn't realise what he was doing, I'd say to him 'No, I haven't quite finished that yet.' He'd say, 'When will you have that done by?' So there were no angry words or anything like that. There was just a recalibration of the completion date. And the third time you got to it again, there was no anger or anything like that, just persistence.

And very often when you tried to drift it out a little too far, you'd hear him say something like 'What about if we could get it done by an earlier time?' Again, you weren't offended by it, but there was a steely determination in him to get the work done. By the third time he'd asked you, you felt embarrassed. Even here he retained the whole concept of leaving things with you, letting you develop the ownership of it and then experiencing the embarrassment of having to be asked three times in a row. I'm not sure if other people felt the same, but I remember once when he'd asked me three times and I was quite determined not to allow that to happen again. I suspect other executives were the same.

In discussing Alan Jeans and Colin Grant, Frank was describing two people whose examples in self-control and quiet, empowering leadership were a formative influence in the development of his abilities. It is interesting to reflect how Frank handled himself in responding to his environment.

A senior colleague of Frank's sheds light on Frank's approach to a time of some crisis for their organisation. When a former major shareholder and Managing Director left the company. The organisation was in a severe liquidity crisis and effectively under the control of some banks. Frank began a series of key meetings with his staff and introduced high levels of personal accountability. In group sessions, he would patiently seek an understanding of each problem area, solicit suggestions, get everyone's feedback, seek agreement as to who would do what and then simply expect the action.

'The process achieved incredible buy-in from people who had never had such direct accountability before,' said Frank's colleague. 'Some opted to leave, but those who stayed achieved terrific focus and a sense of personal responsibility for what had to be done. Some assets had to be sold, overheads had either to be reduced, or significantly refocused on customers, costs and sales — and this and much more was achieved to turn the business around.'

Frank introduced a completely new concept called 'accountability'. 'Up until then everyone had had lots of responsibility, but no real accountability. But he also had a great tolerance for mistakes — as long as the intentions had been well thought out. I made some wrong calls at this time, but on each occasion, when I went in to talk about them', the colleague said, 'he effectively thanked me for the efforts I was making and encouraged me forwards.' Frank is a great believer in principled decision-making: a favourite saying of his is: Let's make a decision on the principles.

We are strongly influenced by example in the early years of our working careers — particularly if we are open to influence from effective people. Frank's case illustrates this pretty well. There is a discernible echo of Frank's early mentors in the way he is described by those around him now.

Susan's responses to questions about early influences were quite different.

What underpins our independence in work is in part the influence of our parents—we have to start here really. My father died when I was ten years old, but he had a strong influence on me in my formative years. He was a hard worker, running various businesses in the fruit markets. He had a degree, but worked in this field, something of a 'Gentleman Jim' in his manner. He was very close to working people. I used to get up at 3 a.m. to make him a cup of tea before he left for work. Work was a very important part of life, but also I saw him respect his staff, look after staff. But also making money was important, as was success.

Then, after his death, I saw my mother initially not cope, but then learn to cope, running the business. She had to pick it up with no real working experience. She was a very feisty woman, whom I admire immensely for her spirit in tackling things, in being independent and growing. She had three tiny children in those years.

I learned that I must always be able to take care of myself. Even in marriages I had to have independence, my own bank account, self-esteem and backing. I early recognised the need to have my own independent financial means and forward planning for all contingencies for the rest of my life.

My first boss was a wonderful woman — very lively, innovative, outspoken, had a real passion about life and work and a very strong set of beliefs. Though I did not share all her beliefs, I respected her, nonetheless. She was a very strong person and a leader who gave me a lot of flexibility: she encouraged me in my own growth. Even though I was only young, she expected me to take responsibility. She was very encouraging and saw my mistakes as learning experiences, not something bad. She had a great sense of humour and a lot of energy.

As Susan reminds us, a lot of pre-conditioning and influencing takes place before we hit organisational life. However, there is not a great deal most of us can do to influence how we are brought up!

*The Titanium Professional* carries a central message of taking charge of your own learning in the work environment. The people, whose comments are captured here — two people who are the embodiment of independence and capability — didn't necessarily start their working lives that way. However, both proved perceptive observers. They are people willing to learn from the example of others. Developing this skill, through self-control, reflection and careful assessment of what others are thinking and doing, is fundamental to building independent capability in yourself.

Not all of us are surrounded by terrific mentors in our early careers, or in subsequent transitions, so we need to build some selection criteria of our own in choosing where to work. A careful assessment of our next 'boss' is very much a part of this.

As Susan and Frank each matured, they became more discerning and critical, able to draw insights and inspiration from 'parts' of people they met. However, it wasn't necessary to adopt the whole approach of influential people around them.

## Formal training and performance appraisal

What of formal training and performance appraisal at work? How significant are they in creating the capabilities of our 'case studies'? Susan, and Ian Greenshields, introduced in Chapter 3 as General Manager Corporate Affairs of a national food manufacturer and distributor, comment here.

Susan:

All through my career I have learnt most through what I have been doing on the job. I have often been teased for not 'training' my staff (that is, sending them off to formal courses), but I think you learn much more on the job. A good working environment, a good boss and useful work is better than a training program. Training supplements and confirms, rather than initiates.

Ian:

Hardly ever has someone sat down and taught me. Performance appraisals, if good, provide confirmation and affirmation. That has been their main (and only) value. When we used to go for medical checks at a time when we were really fit, we knew what the outcome was going to be. We just wanted an affirmation really. Performance appraisals have been like this for me: you know what the outcome is going to be. You are simply getting confirmed things you know.

If something comes as a surprise, in a performance appraisal, you are not in touch with your job, you may not have listened to your supervisor, you have not opened your eyes...

The message is simple — in the business of individual development, those who are independent and capable place self-instruction well ahead of formal training.

## Learning in the workplace?

What did our independently capable professionals find they had to learn at work, beyond the knowledge and skills taught in their school and university days?

Ian:

How the organisation operated — internal information flows, how decisions were reached, external influences and how the organisation dealt with customers or influenced its environment. It is important to understand the wider picture, in which your role is a small part.

Susan:

The application of the learning skills was the big challenge. How do you take intellectual, conceptual learning and apply it in the workplace? I had to learn things like writing, analysis, presentation skills, all the things which are a baseline necessity for administrative work.

Business letters — how to write them — being concise yet not too brusque, recognising that the person receiving them would be busy and getting to the point: this was a skill to be learnt.

In dealing with people, probably the face-to-face aspects were somewhat easier. I had come out of a Phys. Ed. background which prepared me fairly well for this. Perhaps I was a 'natural'. Perhaps I had been surrounded early by so many people who did this well. Then I studied Phys. Ed. which looks at individuals as well as teams — one-to-one and in a group. So I had good one-to-one skills and moved into group and team skills, so the gregarious part wasn't too hard. But this was as a member, not a leader.

Soon I had to learn to deal with people in group situations. I had to learn to manage meetings, to be clear what the meeting was for, put together an agenda and then how to speak to people, how to make verbal presentations.

It was harder to learn the business of managing up and down. This is quite complex. I like differences in people and even eccentric people, even though they may be hard to manage. I like to set an environment that they can achieve in. Early I was dazed by apparent 'brightness' — I didn't find it easy. It is hard when you have subordinates who seem brighter than you. The challenge is to make it a fertile ground for them, but it is important as a boss also to learn from them, to really use them.

Frank talked about timekeeping and self-motivation. He also talked about how knowledge by itself was insufficient. The key was in being able to 'put the rubber on the road,' that is, achieve something with that knowledge through the actions of others.

There is great similarity between these 'survival and growth skills' and several of the Mayer competencies (see Chapter 2) now being addressed in many school curricula, particularly 'working with others and in teams' and 'communicating ideas and information'.

We also see here the need for a lifelong wish to learn, humility, and also a willingness to learn from mistakes rather than retreating from action in fear of making them. Frank again:

> I think you learn by realising you've made a mistake, and admitting you've made a mistake, and saying to yourself you're not going to do that again. You effectively need to be your own worst critic... always looking to improve, always saying: despite the fact that that's turned out well, could I have done it better. And by taking that approach, you can always do it better. Whatever you did yesterday, you can do better tomorrow.

> So it's not only the fact that you can make a real mistake, and I've made plenty of them, it's admitting the fact that you have made that mistake. Having the intestinal fortitude to say, I've buggered that up and then having the ability to move on, not getting yourself down about it. That's yesterday's news, you've got to move on and move on quickly.

This is evidence of self-control and self-management. Independent capability and its development rests very largely on 'being your own teacher and performance appraiser', forming a view of yourself while you learn, and doing this fairly independently of those around you.

## Considering a new career

What advice would our 'case studies' offer someone contemplating a new career?

Frank:

> The first and most important issue is active listening skills: the ability to listen to other people, not necessarily to accept their point of view.

> The second — but a long distant second — is the ability to sell a concept.

> There is also a need for self-confidence — a belief in yourself and in the
> direction or path that you have chosen.

This self-confidence comes across, perhaps, more in the lives and
choices of our two cases than in what they say — though Susan had an
interesting comment:

> You must know 'who' you are, have your own high standards, have a 'sane'
> estimate of your own capabilities. Set out to develop strong relationships
> with carefully selected colleagues with whom you can build trust. Then
> you will draw strength from this, rather than be vulnerable to the approval —
> or disapproval — of others in the organisation.

Where does positive self-talk and self-confidence sit in relation to
our set of critical competencies? It derives from self-control again,
together with initiative. It is something which comes in part from
effective parenting. But it is also a function of constant reinforcement
and is therefore capable of being eroded in the wrong workplace, in the
wrong culture or with poor mentors. People setting out to build
independent capability remove themselves from these environments as
soon as they can.

Being an 'information seeker' seems to be a common characteristic in
these people. The skills of the information seeker derive from our core
capabilities — coming from analytical thinking and initiative/
proactivity. These skills are typically learned ones. We take the initiative,
then discover how to source information about the organisation, its
strategy, current issues affecting it, our competitors, and our regulatory
environment. Independent and capable people ask others to help them
understand financial information, to teach them the significance of
financial ratios and management accounting data, and the like.
Susan:

> The crux of my career was trying to build different experiences. In the
> early years, I was seen by some as being a bit 'flighty' — by changing jobs
> a little too often. But I thought the way to learn was to put myself through
> different learning experiences. I enjoy learning challenges: the climb up
> the hill as it were, not so much being on the top, or the easy life/fruits of
> office, on top or down the other side. I have loved new environments. I

have enjoyed new lessons. I have really enjoyed learning to survive and achieve in new and different environments and then in mastering the challenge. I have worked in big and small organisations, in the private and public sectors and also run my own business.

The attributes you need include being honest and straight. This gives one a resilience, a toughness, an ability to survive. I don't get a high out of playing the corridors of power, playing politics. Go in, use situations to take and absorb new learning and also try to give back and test yourself. Don't just do things in the accepted way: look at the new job with a sense of stretching it in a new way, or in a different way, which contributes more to the organisation. Stretch the role: take it a bit further than the way that is expected: push the boundaries. Do it, even if not encouraged. It doesn't matter if you don't succeed. Look far out and see the fit of the work in the bigger picture. Look for new learning in everything.

## Setting your own goals

Susan, Frank and Ian have had goals of one kind or another at most times in their careers — a picture of what they wanted to be doing and achieving at a point some years ahead. They weren't drifting or being pushed along by their organisations. They had a sense of where they were heading and what experience was needed to get them there.

Frank Whitford admitted a little self-consciously that he drew up plans with his wife — which looked ahead 20 years!

In 1974, I took a view of where my wife and I wanted to be and we actually wrote up some personal goals that we meant to achieve that year. We did it every year for 20 years and we keep a 20-year time frame in front of us each time. I've actually still got the first eight-page document that we wrote in 1974. And we keep that in front of us and we laugh at it now and think how naïve we were when we wrote it. But it was the thing to do... the process which... sent us down the right track.

A 20-year time frame may not suit everyone, but the process of looking to what we should achieve, to what we would like to look back on, seems another common attribute in those who achieve independent capability.

## Summary

These case studies were selected on the basis that Susan, Frank and Ian seemed to embody independent capability. Each was very much in charge of their career and had been so for most of their working life. Their careers reveal the significance of the five core competencies in their lives:

1   self-control and self-management
2   initiative and proactivity
3   ,an ability to empathise — to perceive and understand the feelings of others
4   effectiveness with others, within, and in leadership of teams
5   analytic ability — the ability to assemble, order and interpret data.

Reading their comments, we keep coming across such skills as 'taking charge of your own learning', 'being a perceptive observer', 'learning by doing', and 'learning from mistakes rather than retreating from them'.

The comments reveal the adoption of a range of beneficial operating values and practices in building independent capability. *We build competencies in ourselves by our own practices and values.*

This theme will reappear later in the book, after looking at the lives of other people who have created very different careers for themselves, yet built the same independent capability.

Often, it seems that we drift in our careers, or become swept along in the flow of organisational life. We accept transfers, promotions and changes arising from technology and business activities as given conditions to be assimilated. We buckle under changes in values and behaviours in the leaders of our organisations. We are much more a part of our organisations than we might wish, but we never really question it.

This is certainly not so in our case studies. A restructuring or job change is not seen as a setback. This is a major point in the case for building independent capability. These people are the drivers of their own careers, the causes of their own experience.

In the next chapter, independence and capability outside the context of large organisations are discussed.

# *chapter six*

## Is self-employment the answer?

Many people choose self-employment as the ultimate expression of independence. If they can create some arrangement in which they can earn a good income *and* be their own boss, surely this is pretty close to achieving independent capability?

It can be attractive, certainly, but there are many and varied traps for the unwary. For a great many in small business, the last thing they feel at the end of each day is independent and capable. Of course, for many others, there could be no other choice. For them, it is exactly the right vehicle for independence and self-realisation.

If our ultimate aim is to achieve independence and capability in self-employment, or to use self-employment as a particular vehicle for a limited time, wise decisions need to be made and this choice and its implications need to be understood.

Chapter 6 explores the main issues and some conclusions are reached about the 'self-employment' pathway, and the skills and talents needed for success. In Chapters 7 and 8, case studies illustrate these skills and talents at work.

## The growth of small business and self-employment

Small business is one of the fastest growing areas of employment in many Western economies. Almost by definition, small businesses are begun by people seeking control of their own working lives and an opportunity to build an enterprise themselves.

Small businesses are commonly defined as those employing less than 20 employees in a service industry, or with less than 100 employees in the manufacturing sector.[48] There are approximately 900,000 of these businesses in Australia, according to a recent source.[49] According to the Australian Bureau of Statistics (ABS), this number is growing by more than 200,000 a decade. Their latest overview, 'Small Business in Australia 1997', also records that in a 13-year period up to 1997, total employment in small business grew from

---

[48] Emma Alberici, *The Small Business Book*, Penguin Books, Melbourne, 1995, p. 2.
[49] Tim Colebatch, 'Business on the rise despite the fears.' in *The Age*, 29 May 1998, p. 3, Business Section.

2,163,500 to 3,247,300, creating 54 percent of total job growth in that period.

Some 20–25 percent of executives working through outplacement following their retrenchment from. large organisations in Australia seriously consider becoming self-employed, and as many as half of these do make such a move. Many, of course, look in this direction as a reaction to past stresses and uncertainty in the corporate environments from which they have come. While this may be a good motivation, it is rarely a sufficient one. Many simply see more opportunities in self-employment or with smaller organisations than in rapidly downsizing corporate organisations.

In *How to be a Successful Consultant in Your Own Field*, Hubert Bermont talks of the depression that can come from reflecting on a past organisational career where there has been no fulfilment and little opportunity to be the 'cause of your own experience'. In the introduction, he writes:

*Wherever you are in the table of organisation there is someone or some board taking full charge of your actions or decisions, withholding full credit or compensation for those things you have done expertly and overcharging you for your errors. This authority makes the rules, breaks the rules, changes the rules — sometimes in mid-project. This authority sets standards at will. This authority delegates responsibility, withholds responsibility and accepts responsibility at its own convenience. But most of all this authority offers you and your family a living, or takes it away at will — and therein lies the ultimate power. The threat and the promise, implied or stated.*[50]

Seeing organisational life from this perspective, retrenched executives and those with a fear of control by others leap towards self-employment for its promise of independence and, perhaps, self-actualisation. From this perspective, who could blame them?

A negative reaction to this view of a past or prospective corporate career is understandable, but the premise is debatable. As argued

---

[50] Hubert Bermont, *How to be a Successful Consultant in Your Own Field*, Prima Books, 1997, p. 1.

earlier, there *are* ways to build a career with real independence and capability within organisations and across their boundaries. Professional life is not a 'give up your freedom and work for a large company' or 'achieve nirvana in self-employment' choice at all. You can be free, relatively speaking, in a series of corporate or professional appointments and you can also retain freedom, self-control and integrity when a corporate job is taken away if you have managed to develop independent capability. Managing these transitions is discussed later in this book. It is possible to be trapped on a far worse treadmill in self-employment.

So, despite Hubert Bermont's eloquence in expressing the pain so many experience — pain which is the wellspring of their motivation towards self-employment — this is not a necessary or inevitable reaction to work in larger organisations.

Increasingly, even new graduates look more thoughtfully at smaller organisations and at self-employment against the alternative of joining big organisations. Again, this is a mixture of personal choice and a realistic appraisal of where more fertile opportunities for employment might lie.

For some, self-employment can be a terrific opportunity to develop independence and capability and stands as an attractive path to explore. Being self-employed, in charge of your own enterprise(s), requires a clear understanding of your own strengths and weaknesses, and a comparison of them with the particular aptitudes needed in self-employment. Intelligent self-appraisal is critical: there are no others doing performance appraisals for you. Appraisals and feedback in self-employment come somewhat more brutally in stark financial terms, just a little way into the venture…

In this chapter, those aptitudes and talents usually associated with success in self-employment or in a small business are identified. The core competencies of independent capability are just as fundamental here as on any other pathway. But some particular derivatives of them seem quite critical in self-employment. We might call this a derivative alloy — to stay with the titanium metaphor!

People heading for self-employment usually face a key decision — what form of business should be chosen? Will you sell a service, make a product, start from scratch, buy a business, join with others, purchase a franchise — so the choices unfold.

Next, self-employment requires that people become their own marketing department. They must decide who their customers (the market) will be, and fashion and deliver value for their customers in a form those specific customers find attractive. The sale of services must then deliver some surplus of income over expenditure. In other words, those choosing this path have to develop a viable business concept: again, there is no firm or organisation doing it for you.

There are also a range of straightforward 'commercial' skills to master: the skills of negotiation, networking, time management and organisation. There are essential disciplines and areas of knowledge required in the business of setting up a company: setting up accounts, providing for taxation, complying with regulations, monitoring and managing cash flow and determining the terms of contracts. All sorts of good businesses with profitable goods and services fall over through a lack of attention to what might be called the commercial disciplines of running a business.

It isn't very satisfying to head bravely into self-employment with a sense that one is destined to capture independence and capability if the venture fails in the first year!

The three most common causes of failure in small business, according to the principal of a major accounting group in Melbourne, are lack of capital, insufficient use of legal and financial advice and the absence of commercial or business acumen.[51]

In this chapter, Charles Handy's notion of a 'portfolio career' is also examined. A portfolio career is one in which someone has several 'jobs', that is, more than one source of income and working interest. This is another variation of self-employment and one finding increasing favour among those for whom 'running a business' seems

---

[51] Harvey Cook, of Whelan and Cook, Chartered Accountants, Melbourne.

too hard or unattractive and for whom working in a larger organisation also seems not to be the answer.

## What motivations and talents are required?

In the past few years I have worked with more than 200 people contemplating a move into self-employment and I have followed the progress of their early successes and some failures. Table 6.1 summarises those talents and motivations self-employment requires, drawing largely on their collective experiences.

### Table 6.1 Key requirements of the self-employed

| Attributes and talents | Comments |
| --- | --- |
| Tenacity | Establishing a business, overcoming obstacles, waiting for prospective buyers to make a decision, coping with setbacks and more — tenacity is a critical requirement in successful self-employment. |
| Influencing skills | A mix of communication skills, empathy and tenacity. As a matter of survival, most small business leaders need to influence customers, rental agents, suppliers, lenders and many others in the everyday process of running the business. |
| Integrity | Honesty is basic, yet is sometimes 'honoured in the breach' by some entrepreneurs. Honesty in an inward sense is also critical: being honest about costs, about time invested, being honest with your accountant. Integrity in the numbers is critical in the appraisal of a business and in investing in further development. |

| Attributes and talents | Comments |
| --- | --- |
| **Creativity and flexibility** | Customers never buy exactly as anticipated. The market may not be quite what is expected. The environment changes. Responding with alacrity to market signals is vital in small business operators. |
| **Discipline** | Being focused, allocating necessary time to necessary chores, managing priorities, controlling and allocating expenses, being dedicated to quality, investing in training and delivering against deadlines. |
| **Resourcefulness** | Rarely can one person do all that is required. Effective small business operators tap into all sorts of resources in alliances with other small businesses and other consultants, often on a *quid pro quo* basis, to solve problems creatively. |
| **Commercial acumen** | 'Rat-cunning' might be another term for this! Some people have good business instincts — and some simply haven't. The art seems to be in 'seeing' a service or product for which a market can be created and then bringing the idea into reality with a commercial return attached. If this attribute has not been a part of your repertoire to date, then get good advice and do some 'testing' before making a bet-the-farm decision! |
| **Hunger without greed** | Most small business operators pay themselves relatively little, especially in the early years of their business. They refuse to starve the business of needed working capital. There is a time envisaged when the business will be able to pay a handsome salary or be sold for a gain commensurate with the effort. This is 'hunger' for development of the business, but not 'greed' in terms of early financial reward. |

| Attributes and talents | Comments |
| --- | --- |
| **Maturity, self-control and self-confidence** | Self-confidence and belief in oneself seems critical. Small business or self-employment can be lonely and is not for the faint-hearted or those plagued with self-doubts. Positive self-talk is needed from time to time. |
| **Listening and research skills** | Effective business developers listen carefully — even if some seem to do it in micro-second bursts! At the outset and with each new idea, the marketing key seems to be to carefully research the question: 'Is there a real market for what I plan to do — or is my product one which few people are likely to want?' Energy and ruthless objectivity in appraising what emerges, seem critical — as does the threshold ability of being a good listener. |
| **Clear professional competence in a particular field** | Blindingly obvious? Most people buy the services of a business or a consultancy because the services are ones they cannot easily meet themselves. Even housecleaning services require focus, skill and time management that many of us cannot muster. A clear niche and excellence in that niche is important for successful self-employment. |

There are certainly more aptitudes than these involved, but these are essential. Perhaps as givens, consider good physical and mental health, objectivity and general maturity, courtesy and tact and, of course, the basic ability to analyse the success or otherwise of the venture as it proceeds.

In each of these talents and abilities can be seen the influence of the five elements which deliver independent capability: self-control; proactivity; empathy/listening skills; effectiveness with others; and analytical thinking.

Self-control underpins tenacity, integrity, discipline, maturity (in part) and the ability to be 'hungry but not greedy'. Proactivity and initiative underpin creativity and flexibility. Empathy and listening skills are the foundation of maturity, research skills and the ability to carefully explore the potential of a market. Effectiveness with others is a large part of influencing skills. Clear professional competence and business acumen in the field of self-employment usually rest on developed analytic skills.

The attributes and talents associated with success in self-employment are somewhat more specific, or 'sharper' than the fundamental competencies which make for independent capability in a general sense. But while quite particular talents are needed in self-employment, they are derivatives of the five broader competencies presented in Chapter 2.

## Self-knowledge is vital

As a first step in thinking about self-employment, it is useful to score yourself against a list of attributes such as these. It is important to see where you sit in each of these dimensions or aptitudes and to think carefully if you are fairly low in more than two or three of them.

For the more serious student of this subject, L. and S. Spencer develop a 'Generic Entrepreneur Competency Model' in *Competence at Work*, based on interviews with a great many entrepreneurs and observers of independent business people.

Many people who are self-employed, are *not* talented in all of these things. The key for them is to make an arrangement that covers the gaps. Often entrepreneurs with strength in marketing and business development lack discipline in accounting and administration — and freely acknowledge this gap in their portfolio of skills. Their solution is simply to team up with someone with these skills.

One person I worked with had strong skills and experience in business finance, administration, information systems, process improvement and in the disciplines involved in total quality management. He was attracted to self-employment, but believed that limited experience and undeveloped abilities in selling and persuasion would be his major obstacle. He really did not feel comfortable about selling solutions, or in selling his time and ability in delivering them, to prospective clients.

He teamed up with a two-person consultancy in which the principal had all these strengths — in spades! In fact, the principal typically won more business than he could deliver, so more capability in the business was needed anyway. The new partner brought depth in financial skills and systems which the consultancy lacked. It has proved to be a good partnership. More to the point, my friend now has the confidence to make business presentations and is winning new business for the practice. He has developed confidence and the competencies associated with presenting to and influencing others with the support of his colleague, rather than accepting an earlier limitation.

Those who succeed in self-employment acknowledge and manage their businesses to cover their 'gaps' or limitations. Often essential talents and attributes can be acquired through an alliance of one form or another.

Sometimes would-be entrepreneurs are highly talented in a field — it might be computer-based publishing, for example — and the problem that arises might be a function of days spent immersed in the 'doing' (on the computer in this case), with insufficient time spent listening hard to customers and marketing. This problem may be one of a lack of balance in skills and preferences: too much weight on some attributes at the expense of others. Such a difficulty reinforces the need for discipline in managing time and focus.

There is another important aspect to self-knowledge if you intend to become self-employed — thinking about what you need in order to remain cheerful and sustained as a person.

One 'archetypal entrepreneur' I have been counselling is extremely bright in the field of financial intermediation and has the ability to pull off an endless number of financial deals between those who need equity funding and those who look for opportunities to invest in growing businesses. The prospect of doing this independently beckons, with financiers keen to have him around working on a commission basis. However, the one issue which needs discussion and reflection in his life is the need he has for plenty of team interaction. He believes that he is at his best surrounded by others in regular office contact, with the cut and thrust of exchanges with colleagues, and perhaps some of the checks and balances of a regular organisation. It is a genuine need that is clearly influencing his thinking, as it should.

There are others, of course, for whom the measure of isolation and independence which often comes with self-employment is a gift, a terrific opportunity to satisfy their own need for space and autonomy. So, although it might seem obvious, think about what you need in your working life. What environment works best for you, and can you create this in your anticipated version of self-employment?

## Choosing the right business

The next test of self-employment as a career comes in the choice of business. There are a range of decisions: start one from scratch? Buy one? Buy part of one with an equity investment? Invest in a franchise? Establish a consultancy? Join others in a boutique consultancy?

Each of these decisions is surrounded by an array of tests. For example, the great advantage of buying a business is that there is a track record to study. The tests come in a comprehensive 'due diligence' appraisal: the careful assessment of the quality of existing revenue, current indebtedness and forward commitments, guarantees and liabilities, information systems, supplier relationships and loyalty, and so on.

Cold-start enterprises entail much greater risk. According to Emma Alberici's *The Small Business Book,* some 50 percent of small businesses fail by their second year and 75 percent fail in the first three years.[52]

## Franchising

Franchising presents lower risks. According to the Deputy Chairman of the Franchising Council of Australia (FCA), there are some 30,000

---

[52] Alberici, pp. 80, 195.

franchisees in Australia and this number is growing at the rate of 14 percent a year. Franchising is currently 2.5 times more likely to succeed than an independent business.[53] However, while franchising appears safer for the would-be independent business person, it is not for everyone. Franchisees must follow precisely a set business system — albeit one likely to have been thoroughly road-tested by the franchisor — and the qualities sought in them include absolute discipline in adherence to the system. Franchisees also need to be excellent with people, both customers and staff, and able to work very long hours in duplication of a successful operating formula.

Franchising is not for the entrepreneur who wants to invent new products and services, to diversify, or to chase a new market or geographic area.

The Deputy Chairman of the FCA again:

**Franchising combines the best of big business (branding, marketing, systems, strategy and research and development) with the best of small business (owner operator's enthusiasm, customer service, hard work and attention to detail).[54]**

However, for all its lower risk, buying a franchise entails running some tests as well. Perhaps the most important is a look at the books of an available franchise, if there is one, or oversight of the business results of other franchises in the group. Other tests include careful assessment of the franchisor and of the value the franchisor will offer on an ongoing basis. The franchise agreement should be independently appraised by your lawyer for any unreasonable financial burdens, conditions to apply on exit, requirements to purchase set products at set prices, and the like. Further issues to review include the rights of the franchisee to a 'territory' or defined customer base, the duration of the franchise and renewal options.

---

[53] Mark Abernethy, 'FCA Rejects Franchise Slowdown Claim.' in *Australian Financial Review*, 13 January 1998, p. 18, Small Business section.
[54] David Acheson, Deputy Chairman, Franchise Council of Australia, in a letter to the editor, *Australian Financial Review*, 30 December 1997, p. 12.

## Consulting

'Consulting' is a somewhat misunderstood label, which increasingly covers the business of providing services in some area that larger organisations wish to outsource. Thus the outsourcing of recruitment, outplacement, reconfiguring information systems, studying new strategic choices, publishing brochures and many other activities usually entail commissioning 'consultants'.

The term 'consultant' should more properly be confined to people who work within organisations as facilitators, catalysts, designers of processes: people with the skills to cause others to act, people with the ability to embed skills in organisations. However, the term is increasingly applied to all manner of activities which might better be described as 'outsourced service providers', were this description not so clumsy!

An ever widening array of services are now delivered under the general term of consulting — and I am continually fascinated by their range. Consulting is a vehicle for a great deal of the new 'work' discussed in earlier chapters. As an example, under the recent growth of specialist 'relocation consultants' (who help manage interstate and overseas transfers of staff) there are niche service delivery businesses in 'unpacking and house set up' operations and in 'cultural awareness and sensitivity training' for those going overseas. In the world of financial services, one category of consultants are those who broker and negotiate major lending between banks and businesses needing capital for expansion. There are now niche consultants offering such services — and a range of intermediation activities — for smaller companies as well. There are literally hundreds of services now outsourced to specialist consultants — and many of these are self-employed people.

There are significant implications in the choices between sole consulting, consulting with three or four partners in a boutique business and consulting with a large consulting group. These include the proportion of income retained (as opposed to being applied to overheads), the winning of business (which is much harder in the sole practice situation where initially there is no 'name' or reputation to attract customers) and the issue of reciprocal obligations to partners and income assignment in those businesses which involve more than one person.

## Alliances

Much work comes about through temporary alliances with others. Initially, I thought I should keep my consulting focus to myself — or at least confine my explanation of it to potential customers. Sharing my ideas and thoughts with other consultants seemed akin to leaking vital intellectual capital. Well, that turned out to be a foolish notion. Whether my offerings were particularly bright or not was beside the point: no-one else could replicate my experience and preferences, even if they sought to. More importantly, if I shared my interests with others, quite often they would win work for which my interests and abilities would add value, or I might win a project and need their help. Sole consultants constantly experience the 'feast or famine' dilemma — more work than they can handle some of the time and not enough at other times. Alliances are a terrific means to help each other out and be helped.

The key to forming alliances with other self-employed people is networking. The significance and skills of networking in self-employment will be discussed shortly. However, here it should be noted that networking skills are critical in the business of building and sustaining alliances with other consultants.

The bottom line is that for most self-employed people their vocation is not a vehicle for retreating from relationships with others: their business will *require* greater focus on networking than was ever required in former corporate lives. Effectiveness with other people, one of the five fundamental competencies, is nearly always critical for the self-employed.

## Defining and testing the business concept

A fundamental element in choosing one of these careers is the issue of the business concept. What exactly is the service or product and who will be the customers? How will they see value in the service or product? If they are other businesses, how will it help them win and profit from their customers? How will it be different and more attractive than the offerings of others?

These are fundamental questions — yet it is surprising how many people I see about to embark in the direction of setting up a business, even a consulting practice, without addressing them carefully. As Michael Gerber remarks in *The E-Myth*:

*The entrepreneurial model does not start with a picture of the business to be created, but of the* customer *for whom the business is to be created. It understands that without a clear picture of that customer, no business can succeed.*[55]

What many do is identify something they like doing and which they do well, perhaps something they feel ought to be purchased by others. They then move quickly into commitments, financial and personal, in structuring a business around their picture of what they will do before checking whether there are real customers for this service.

## Steps for testing your concept

Concept testing is a precursor to marketing and the very real business of winning customers. It establishes whether there is first-level interest in what the business or service will deliver and determines the language that should be used in putting the proposition to the market. People contemplating self-employment should work through the following steps:

1 Write down on one, or at the most two pages some summary paragraphs covering:
— what the business offering is, or what the customer gains from the service
— how this is delivered
— who you are (that is, establish your credibility)
— what your service or product will cost.

---

[55] Michael E. Gerber, *The E-Myth*, Harper Business, US, 1986, p. 43.

Your headings might be:

— Organisations which use our services achieve…

— We build this ability for them by…

— We bring experience in…

— Our costing is developed as follows….

2 Go out to 'test' the description of this concept with respected, objective, experienced people who are ideally 'like' your prospective customers. Begin by saying something like 'I am thinking of establishing a business: tell me how you feel about this concept.' Then stop talking and listen hard to their reactions!

3 In the light of the reactions you receive, refine your statement again and test it again with someone else. Listen hard to the 'Yes, but…' reactions, and really refine your offering and the language in which it is described to best match the interests of those you are meeting. Repeat the process until you get the 'Aha… this looks interesting…' reaction, or other clearly positive signals that your concept statement appears to represent an attractive business offering.[56]

Often people contemplating self-employment are fixed closely to what they want to do, or make, and they describe it in *their* language, with *their* perspectives. It is often difficult to move out of your own heads into those of people like customers, yet until you can describe something in the language of prospective customers, triggering a customer's 'hot buttons', the chances are that your business offering won't be easy to sell.

This is termed concept testing, but it is also 'proximity testing', a term used by marketing specialists. The people who take the trouble to do this begin to get a sense of whether there is a market for their business. It is also why it is critical that concept testing is undertaken with experienced business people who are most like prospective customers. Concept testing with friends and relatives just does not provide the hard feedback necessary.

---

[56] My initial insights here were inspired by the advice of Frederick Davidson, Chairman of RightD&A (formerly known as Davidson and Associates), a major Australasian career transition consultancy.

In summary, concept testing is all about establishing:

- whether a business concept is clear to others
- whether what is being described is something that prospective customers will respond positively to
- whether there is likely to be a *market* for what is planned.

Concept testing is not rocket science and it is not expensive. But it is an essential first step before too many irrevocable steps are taken down the path of self-employment. The process is difficult and takes — here we go again — a measure of tenacity and good listening skills. The difficulty resides mostly in moving from *your* language to the language of customers. Some people can't or won't attempt this: if they can't discipline themselves to think their business idea through, get it down in writing and discuss it with people like prospective customers, perhaps self-employment is not a great choice for them.

Of course, there *are* successful entrepreneurs who haven't done this. Many, however, go through a number of trial and error start ups, often at some expense in time and cost before succeeding. For those who are making a 'bet the farm' decision, concept testing is a fundamental first step. Business start-up does not have to be a baptism of fire due to avoidable mistakes.

Concept statements, once refined and eliciting positive responses, become the basis of marketing documentation and verbal presentations a little further down the path.

## Marketing

When a business concept appears viable, the next step is to create or move into the market for the services or products. Marketing is founded on listening and discovery (which begin with concept testing) and is built up on effective communication. It requires you to target prospective customers and to reach them in the right form with offerings that represent value to them. Approaches might be through advertisement, the publication of articles and newsletters, or directly.

Networking is the most effective marketing medium for small service businesses. Networking is the process of forming mutually beneficial relationships with current and prospective customers. Networking means meeting, asking questions of and helping other business associates. Networking is *not* selling. Networking is taking a healthy interest in the challenges of other business people and gathering intelligence. It involves an exchange of value, with advice, perhaps. Sometimes your interest in others coincides with the opportunity to provide the services of your business.

Cold calling, advertisements and direct selling have a place at the fast moving consumer goods (FMCG) end of the market but for most other forms of small business, relationship marketing, or networking, seems more effective.

Marketing is often confused with selling. Marketing is much more about listening than telling. It is discovering what organisations or people will buy — sometimes influencing or crystallising a need where one hasn't previously been understood to exist — and then establishing whether the price customers might pay will cover all the costs involved plus a profit.

Marketing in the context of consulting should also be seen as much more a process of seeing and delivering *solutions* than promoting a 'product'. An associate has said:

*Think of a day in the life of the chief executive, or whoever you will be talking to, think about the sorts of issues and problems they wrestle with and then think of how you might be able to assist materially with solutions for one or more of them...*

The expression: 'This looks like a solution looking for a problem', is now quite common. Yet this is precisely how many small businesses — and consulting businesses — are conceived and then fail. They are product driven. The key to marketing is to get into the heads and daily lives of those with whom you hope to interact commercially and then to create solutions for their problems.

## Basic commercial disciplines

*The Titanium Professional* does not cover all of the requirements for success in small business — nor is it the purpose of the book. There

are hundreds of books which cover this field — I have mentioned
Emma Alberici's book *The Small Business Book* — but there is another
of the 'starter pack' variety which I also enjoyed. This is Ann-Maree
Moodie's book, *Small Poppies.*[57] There are good messages in both for
people setting up their own businesses, fully supported by a wealth of
vignettes and case studies. One of the themes which kept emerging
between the lines in Ann-Maree Moodie's book was how hard most of
her case studies had had to work to get their enterprises up and going.
Self-employment is usually very hard work. A qualification here is that
it is *self-directed* hard work and, somehow or other, this does not seem
as stressful.

Managing the 'nitty-gritties' of small business — getting on top of
basic commercial disciplines — should, however, be mentioned.

It's not necessary to be an accountant because accountants can be
approached for advice and services. It's not necessary to be a lawyer —
again, their advice can be sought. But it *is* necessary to know when to
call on such people, to put intelligent and well thought-out business
concepts to them for examination and advice and, most importantly,
to listen to their advice. Small business operation usually necessitates
taking a step up from the corner store tax accountant who may have
served a PAYE client well in the past to someone with a portfolio of
small business clients and solid commercial experience.

Most of those who are successfully self-employed have become
familiar with basic commercial disciplines such as having and
operating a set of accounts, assimilating taxation and the regulations
and obligations flowing around payrolls, insurance, fringe benefits and
superannuation. Generally, use is made of simple computer-based
software in managing these things. And if you aren't good at these
things — as in my case — you need to cover the gap.

Most important is reflection on the financial fundamentals of
business activities. Ask yourself what income will flow from your
efforts, what the timing of the income flows will be, what the
associated costs and their timing will be and what these cash flows

---

[57] Ann-Maree Moodie, *Small Poppies*, Prentice Hall, Sydney, 1996.

mean in terms of your ability to survive. What working capital is needed to start with? What will also be needed through the cycles of the business (taking a conservative view of the likely ebbs and flows of income and expenses)? And then, stepping back from this, what is the overall contribution of the work and the return on investments — is this business a viable one? In quite a few small businesses — guest houses come to mind — the principals do survive but at effective hourly rates well below what they could earn in regular employment. If there are lifestyle issues involved, maybe the balance is a good one — but you should certainly do your sums beforehand.

Business and financial planning, especially building a cash-flow forecast, comprises the process of internally testing a business. This starts with the construction of a marketing plan in which you are forced to write down who your customers are expected to be, how you will communicate with them (and what this will cost), what they will receive, what it will cost to deliver, how you will be different from others and how you will be effective in achieving sales.

Next, this picture is translated into a cash flow — in which the cost and timing of outgoings are set against income and the expected timing of income. Again, assumptions are forced into the open — to the harsh glare of a written plan. The point of these exercises is to see what the real implications of the business are in financial terms and to expose those assumptions to a bit of reality testing.

Recourse to respected and experienced business, accounting and legal advisers is prudent at this point. It seems that many would-be entrepreneurs are so filled with the uniqueness of their plans and so reluctant to have others prick their balloons that many businesses start and fall over through the absence of independent advice in the early stages.

The advice of a good friend made some years ago suggested that intelligence is best measured not by the innate cleverness of an individual, but by the much greater wisdom of learning to listen to others and to seek advice when one's own experience is limited. He was referring, of course, to emotional intelligence, which we discussed in Chapter 2. Successful small business operation requires plenty of this, especially in seeking and listening to others in gaining commercial acumen.

Some people focus on the axioms that small business requires hard work, tenacity and customer focus to the exclusion of other things. The view is that, whatever the obstacle, hard work will see them through adversity. The 'other things' (that I believe to be essential) include thinking hard about the real needs of customers and having the good sense to seek advice — to use external sounding boards. The 'other things' rest substantially on maturity, listening skills and self-control, which sounds like a familiar refrain.

Being successful in commercial terms also requires judgment in such areas as matching costs to affordability, starting off modestly, perhaps out of a home office rather than leasing expensive premises, and in using casual support services for secretarial and printing work on a variable rather than a fixed cost basis. Good judgment is also required in carefully defining what you can and cannot do for clients, in targeting work which you can do effectively and which will generate a fair return and declining work which won't meet both criteria. Good judgment means being flexible and delivering to clients what they want from you, rather than what you might prefer to sell. It means locating and using effective alliances with others; it means striking the right balance in pricing your products and services.

Being self-employed requires all of the attributes identified with being independent and capable and can provide a terrific vehicle for sustaining them. But self-employment tests these attributes more rigorously than regular employment and requires in addition a range of skills and knowledge not always acquired by the regular transition through schools, university and employment.

## 'Portfolio' careers

In *The Age of Unreason* and in subsequent books, Charles Handy examines the increasing popularity of a *portfolio* of work for many people. These people may work in two or more part-time interests, perhaps combining a part-time job here with some consulting there and some teaching in evenings, perhaps at a local TAFE. Increasingly, some people opt to work at a variety of activities and are being quite sufficiently remunerated for them — but without being on any particular organisation's payroll.

In *Making Your Future Work*, Marcus Letcher explores this approach in some detail. He talks of 'modular work', suggesting that care ought to be taken to build the right combination of 'core' activity and 'gap fillers'.

This is an attractive approach for many, but it requires at least some of the disciplines associated with setting up and running an actual business. People doing this need to test the viability of the business concept of each activity carefully. Ask exactly what will be the value to others in this work. Will there be a price paid which provides fair reward after the costs involved in delivering this service? How will revenue be won and what will be the best medium and cost of making sales? What are the cash flows arising from each of the bits of the portfolio? Is the probable volatility attached to some or all of them manageable?

A portfolio career where each of the activities is of a modest character is probably not a wise choice if you have a substantial mortgage and a brace of school fees to sustain. But this choice can be quite liberating at a time in one's career when these things are no longer priorities.

A portfolio can also be useful if you are exploring several business options: you may try three things and see which is the most fun and the most rewarding financially; then focus in this area.

For most of us, the focus and discipline required in our primary profession or activity are as much as we can muster in the working hours of each day. The ability to switch gear and work with other sets of customers in multiple enterprises is not given to everyone.

It is important to step back and look at the bigger picture. This means asking whether self-employment is a better vehicle than most others for achieving independence and capability — considering all the issues we have now covered.

There are many people in self-employment who would hardly

describe their condition as feeling independent and capable. People in this circumstance are all around us, running small enterprises all day and every day, working long hours for meagre rewards and clearly 'trapped' in the enterprise.

Many authors also focus on the need to step back if you are running your own business, to work *on* the business rather than *in* the business. Your aim ought to be to create systems and capabilities in the business and its staff, so that it runs itself most of the time. Your task, your objective as the owner/developer, should be to work on issues of growth, new product development and the like.

Gerber picks up this subject well in *The E-Myth*. He suggests that in starting an enterprise you should ask yourself what your goal is to be doing and experiencing in five years. If getting up early and making Millie's Cookies 12 hours a day is not what you want to be doing five years from now, don't buy a Millie's Cookies franchise! If the reality of the enterprise is that you will be trapped doing the every day tasks of the business 12 hours each day at that five-year point, then maybe this is not such a wise choice after all.

Self-employment, then, doesn't guarantee the achievement of independence and capability. It can be a great vehicle for someone with the insights and breadth of talents and capacities we've discussed. For many living through corporate downsizing and outsourcing, it is the only choice. For them, the process of building a new career around self-employment is liberating and a fresh challenge. Self-employment is increasingly being considered by recent graduates. The challenges they face are perhaps greater (in the absence of commercial experience) but the risks are also mitigated by their generally greater willingness to try new ideas and to bounce back after adversity.

Self-employment also has traps for the unwary. The likely absence of corporate politics and bureaucracy as a limiting condition may simply be replaced by the unrelenting grind of having to continually win more customers.

In the next chapter, two case studies are reviewed illustrating very different types of self-employment.

## Summary

The ideas on self-employment that we have covered in this chapter are summarised below.

- Self-employment can be a vehicle for achieving independence and capability, but it is not axiomatic that this state will always be delivered.
- Self-employment does require particular aptitudes—all of which are derivatives of the five competencies which sustain independent capability. If there are gaps in these aptitudes, the next important issue is working out how to cover them in alliances with others, or in retained resources.
- There are many types of small business and each has implications which should be examined carefully.
- The new business concept must be carefully explored and tested. Key questions to ask include: What value will I deliver? Who will be my customers? Why will they choose me ahead of others?
- Networking is of fundamental significance for most small businesses in winning customers.
- Successful self-employment requires, or develops, much broader knowledge, or perhaps more general business acumen, than regular employment.
- A portfolio of different forms of work is another variant of self-employment which is attractive for many, but still carries with it the need to win work and manage multiple sets of customers.

# *chapter seven*

## Case studies in self-employment

This chapter looks at two case studies of self-employed people who have developed independently capable careers, Trevor Sinclair and Richard Panelli.

## Introducing Trevor Sinclair and Richard Panelli

Trevor is the principal of The Consulting Resources Group. At the time of our initial discussions, the Group had 15 employees and annual revenues fluctuating around a median of just over $4 million. Trevor has since downsized his business and made some other changes mentioned later.

Trevor explained the focus of his business:

> We typically work with major corporations at times of significant change in products, services or more particularly in marketing and distribution channels. It is a time (within the organisation) of fundamental questioning of the relevance of its offer and of the way it goes to market. We assist them in research and in thinking, in conceptualising new approaches to marketing and then in the translation of such new strategies into programs of activity in the organisation. We assist to communicate and embed new disciplines: to bring about the whole gamut of changes needed to operationalise their new marketing approach.

Richard currently owns and runs a small business making dog kennels, cubby houses, rabbit hutches and other wooden products for homes. At the time of our first conversation, he employed one part-time person. The turnover is between $150,000 and $200,000 per annum at present. Richard has plans to significantly increase the size of the business.

Distribution and marketing of Richard's products occurs through hardware and garden supplies businesses, with which Richard works closely to achieve mutually beneficial outcomes.

Richard bought this business after 23 years with a major banking organisation and a career built largely as an internal trainer and training manager. The trigger to make the move was his retrenchment — although for many years he had enjoyed woodwork and nursed the idea of setting out on his own.

While Trevor's consulting focus is distinctive and a little unusual, his business epitomises boutique management consulting. Richard also runs a business which is not atypical among small manufacturing enterprises. These two case studies in self-employment represent businesses of which there are many thousands, in various shapes and sizes. Chapter 8 looks at people who have created quite new niches for themselves, activities without much in the way of precedent.

## The consultant

Trevor Sinclair has an unusual personality, even in the world of consulting, for someone actively working in major corporations. He operates out of an office in one of the more cosmopolitan areas of Melbourne, where staff move with easy informality through his large office, comprised essentially of a large table and a whiteboard. Trevor is more often than not in casual clothes. He has a rich sense of humour, with wide interests in theatre and cinema. In 'work' discussions, he is restless, highly creative and inclined to the use of diagrams and models to facilitate discussions of situations, change and strategy. This is coupled with a great interest in other people and their ideas. Trevor is an excellent listener, with the skill of encouraging others to talk before offering his own insights.

He explained that an early decision to study aeronautical engineering was driven more from a desire to avoid going to a university in Brisbane (at the time this degree was only available in Melbourne) and a desire to avoid the more conventional vocations which appeared then as the only alternatives. Trevor enrolled in an airforce-funded degree course.

During his degree, through days spent in a library with a girlfriend, Trevor picked up and read the works of Freud and from there developed an interest in psychology. His decision to study psychology then had several implications: he undertook the first year of a psychology degree while doing the final year of engineering and then had to pay off a substantial bond to the airforce to avoid six years of service.

He completed the degree in psychology while working part time with a large insurer in their human resources department. When the degree was finished, together with postgraduate training in counselling, Trevor had decided that he did not have a strong interest in a corporate career. He went to the Chief Sales Manager of the organisation and, as he puts it:

> I made my first pitch as a consultant. I said: 'You have some quite serious problems in your area. I would like to put to you a proposal to fix them up over a two-year period.'

Trevor won the project — albeit as a staff member on a salary rather than as a fee-based consultant.

> But after twelve months of this I realised that my real interest lay in consulting and I raised the notion that I would leave to do this. His response was to double my salary — to my complete amazement — and to persuade me to stay on for another year. I did, but only for this extra year. He was very good, providing me with overseas exposure and an opportunity to look at the same issues I was working on in the UK, in continental Europe and in South Africa.

> But by then I was embarked — mentally at least — on a career in consulting and I did not give another thought to staying on in a corporate environment. I left at the end of the year I had promised the Chief Sales Manager.

> I joined up with a fellow I had done counselling training with. He was then working in recruitment and psychological counselling — but my slant was more towards career development, performance appraisal, training and development.

> I have to say that with not much thought then to a product or a proposition, we started working through Yellow Pages cold calling. It amuses me that our first client was Australian Consolidated Industries (ACI) and then our next was Australian Petrochemical Corporation (APC) — and soon after came British Petroleum (BP).

> What we would try and do is get into situations where we could see someone addressing a need for organisational change of some scope — someone with a vision who needed help. But the nature of our help was more or less invented or created by each situation. We liked to start from

a clean sheet of paper and a series of challenges and try to do something dramatically better than what had been done before, largely by going back to a careful diagnosis of the present and then of how to get to a different future. We did not take a package or a solution from anyone: most assignments started from that blank sheet of paper.

You could argue that Trevor had a very unclear business concept! You might also argue that you don't need one if you have a clear focus — in this case a focus on managing change — and a great deal of intelligence and consulting ability. It might also be said that gaining an entry today, with as broad a proposition as Trevor had some years ago, is much more difficult than it was then.

Trevor's consulting business was very successful very quickly, probably testimony to his mix of intelligence, creativity and listening skills. During the next few years he grew the practice, mostly through referrals, but took three-month 'sabbaticals' as well, using one to study drama at university.

Then I did a bit of reappraisal of career direction and started looking at what were emerging trends which might be interesting to follow where we had transferable skills. This led to a focus on predictions about the high growth of franchising. I did a whistle-stop tour, meeting a number of leaders in this area in the US and this led to us joining the Franchise Architects company based in Chicago in an alliance.

Over the next few years, Trevor focused his efforts on assisting emerging businesses to implement franchises, taking up equity in a number of the businesses involved. This led to a really dramatic growth phase in the firm, taking it from three or four people to some 34 staff at one time.
However:

What we rapidly discovered was that the more successful we were in sponsoring and investing in these businesses, the more difficult it was to manage and achieve positive cash flow. You cannot sustain growth without lots of cash and we soon had every asset hocked. We weren't drawing any money ourselves but we were being written up in the business media as a great success!

We decided to list on the second board and started the process of drawing up a prospectus and getting underwriting and so on. I don't quite know what triggered my next decision, but I then suddenly thought about what this might mean. I thought about the implications of becoming a public officer of a company which was listed and in a growth phase, with all the attendant difficulties. This effectively meant going back to being an employee. The implications were not at all attractive. So we changed direction and went through the fairly messy business of selling these businesses off. At the end, the outcome was that we had effectively made no return on some three years of work. The bulk of the employees went with the businesses being sold.

I then decided to return to consulting to the big corporate sector—but now with very much a channel marketing and distribution focus. There had been huge learnings about what it takes to get new divisions or product lines on their feet in the franchising period. We went back to the corporate sector, with the proposition really about using a marketing approach to channels, but drawing back to the previous approach of working alongside managers and using the consulting skills we had developed earlier on.

Trevor has grown the consulting practice, with offices now in Sydney as well as in Melbourne, with his new focus. Clients have included major insurance companies and retailers addressing major shifts in marketing strategy and in organisational structure. Trevor's approach is still one of 'taking blank sheets of paper' — usually a whiteboard — and mapping present realities, options, paths to alternate positions and implications. Their work is with, rather than for, managers and their process entails some rigour in assembling research, documentation, systems and training which will lead to the desired change.

Trevor was asked how he might hire a successor and the attributes he would be looking for. (This was a way of avoiding asking what he felt his competencies were — but getting to the same point!)

If I was to hire a successor, the overriding thing to look for would be an ability to look at a situation and then to be able to draw a line from there to somewhere more positive. An awful lot of people can be stumped by what looks to be an impasse and don't know what to do. The reality is that there is no straight line to a better position, the first and instinctive reaction needs to be one of taking a blank sheet of paper, capturing the present situation and then to start envisioning the line out. What is it that is stopping things, break the thinking impasse, thinking laterally. I need a predisposition to see every event as a launching pad for some productive action.

This means in most instances that we need to sit down and do the thinking and perhaps some research — but you are immediately in the mode of thinking of pathways onward and out. The elegance of the solutions we have come up with for many clients doesn't reveal the amount of pain which went on behind in the thinking and analysis stages.

We need a tenacity, a mental discipline — you don't walk away. But we also need to avoid getting into the setback. This is often the moment in which you win the client forever. Their view is that they are somewhat trapped at that time. This is our moment of opportunity and we must make it happen. We also focus on implementation rather than any one 'product' or tactic to be sold. We are focused on commercial outcomes, not the elegance of our own thinking.

My role also requires an attention to detail — which I suppose others would not always see. I have always enjoyed the aspect of pulling back to see the big picture and the processes of firing up people's imagination — but it is also the obligation of the principal of the business to be focused on detail. I won't let any document leave this place for a client without going over it. I have to be focused on quality and quality control. This is not an option.

I suppose another criterion for my successor is that the person has to be outcome focused. We can have a terrific 'high' in the business when a major project is finished and the client is delighted with the outcome — but we have then to pick ourselves up and work on the next. This gets back to the focus of the principal again. Some of my staff inevitably want to wind down and relax for a few months before winding themselves up into the next project- but I cannot afford to have this occur. Often, all that I have wanted too is to wind down, take a break and so on, but I cannot: I have to bring energy levels up and get a focus on the next project.

Another revealing comment came when Trevor was asked about the personal implications of the career he had built.

Running your own business is sometimes the right to work 24 hours a day, seven days a week and there have been times I have done that. I think there are odd times when the fact of the responsibility coming back to you can be quite daunting. Perhaps at the end of the year, when you need a break and a recharge — these are the times when you wish you had someone standing behind you to carry on activities. It is hard to match the enthusiasm of people embarking on new projects sometimes — yet it is your task to build the rhythms of the business and to create the new waves of energy at the times they are required. It can be hard if your own work and life rhythms are out of step with the needs of the business. A large part of what we sell is energy.

Finally, Trevor is now moving into what may be the 'final' career platform for him. It arises from the essential vulnerability of consulting.

Probably the main vulnerability of consulting businesses is that they have no trailing revenue streams. While you may have had 20 years in consulting when you have had continuity of assignments and income, you have no guarantee that next year will deliver the same.

One line of business now being built is a distribution business in financial services and advice.

For a time now, we have had some transferable skills where we could have built businesses and yet what we have ended up doing is work for which we have charged one-off fees only. Our current aim is to get some leverage off the intellectual property and skills we have built and delivered to our clients. In one exercise we did last year, we delivered $200 million to the bottom line of our client in about seven or eight months and it cost them $1.2 million. Our view is that this is not a particularly good return to us. A merchant banker would not work this way. We are not driven by income, but by the choices the way you work gives you —and we need to change things.

Trevor has now reduced the size of his business and is building alliances to increase the ability of his firm to add e-commerce and IT-enabled marketing to the strategy discussion they undertake with clients. Two principal alliances have been formed — one with a major IT and software organisation and the other with a specialist in new outsourced services, such as call centres. The further possibility exists of creating a new venture to deliver a range of outsourced services — a vehicle which may list on the stock exchange.

Had he the chance to redesign his career, what would Trevor have changed?

> I have never contemplated working in a corporate life. My need for control, or my perceptions around this are critical to me. You could argue that in particular assignments for particular clients I am at their beck and call — but I don't see it that way. When I am very frustrated with a particular client, I say to myself, when they wake up each morning, they will still be looking at themselves — whereas I may have moved on.

> My idea of hell would be being a Chief Executive of a major corporation. Their companies ask too much. The demands even extend into their personal lives and spaces and I could not cope with this. The costs for me would be too high. I have had a major impact on aspects of company activities, but I do get to move on.

What conclusions can be drawn from all this? Trevor is someone clearly strong in self-control, in listening skills, proactivity, effectiveness with people and in analysis at a number of levels. Trevor embodies independent capability. Beyond these fundamental competencies, his story also illustrates several of the sharper competencies, or derivatives, which sustain self-employment. These include great flexibility as his business focus changed, tenacity, influencing skills, resourcefulness and commercial acumen.

The model of independent capability is naturally no guarantee of continuous business success. For all his formidable strengths, Trevor's consulting business has had its reversals and shifts in direction. However, Trevor's approach in these transitions simply illustrates the value of the underlying competencies discussed. He has built on his experience and ultimately had a rewarding and full career.

## The self-employed manufacturer

Richard Panelli has recently made a very different career move. For someone in his early 40s, with three young daughters, the move has been a courageous one. What prompted it?

Redundancy was really a means to an end. For five to six years I had wanted to get out on my own. The redundancy made me do something about this. I wanted to do it on my own [become self-employed] and to prove that I did not need the corporate world to support me. I wanted to build my own empire. Having worked 23 years in the one organisation—[I felt] it was always working for someone else: at the end of the day you were doing what 'they' wanted. Although in the last 10 to 15 years I had had a fair bit of autonomy, I still had the oversight of 'big brother' as it were: either supporting you or putting constraints on you.

I was attracted to creativity in self-employment. The world is your oyster as far as lateral thinking and creativity is concerned. It is up to you to determine which way you want your organisation to go, what you want it to achieve. I see in 12 months time my business could look very different to what it is now. It could have a different clientele and different products. This will be the outcome of my lateral thinking and productivity.

Woodworking has always been a favourite pastime for me. Even when I was working with the bank in the early stages, I had a part-time job making lace-top fences, probably earning more than I was in the bank at that time. Timber also lends itself to being creative.

I bought an existing business being run by a fencer. In doing the due diligence, I checked over the figures, including product volumes. I also had my accountant look at this. I reference-checked the person and the business via contacts. I had to find out what the business was like, what the debts were and so on. I did not want to buy a business where people did not want to deal with me, where I could not get supplies or distribute product because of an adverse reputation.

I use hardware shops and garden suppliers as my main outlets. I have run a new product line past them — in the line of garden arches and gate houses and that sort of thing and their response has been How soon can you get it to me? — which is encouraging.

The hardware and garden supplier shops sell the products. Some of them hold stock and others display stock with me replacing it from time to time. They get me to deliver to them, unless their end customer wants installation. We do installations and assemblies, but we do charge separately for this.

I grow revenues by making sure I have the right product at the right time. I do have a current dilemma in that supplies of the low-cost timber I use for the kennels are drying up. I am not going to keep supplying this product range if the sources of timber used in the past dry up and sales of the kennels become uneconomic. In the gardenware-type products, capturing markets is important — being in there with the right product before others, making sure you are selling quality product (not always the cheapest) and being aware where there might be demand for another product.

Everything going well, I would like to get a display into the House and Garden exhibition in Melbourne in the next couple of years. I have heard stories of how people have gone in, set up a stall and gone then from being a local industry to being a national industry.

Effectively, we rest on the marketing of the retailers, their position in shopping centres and their other products 'pulling' customers past my products. I set up my products in the outlets and show them how they should be displayed. Before I line up another retailer, I check up on their location and make sure they are not going to impinge on the market of a retailer I might be using in the same area. I am very conscious of giving clients room to be able to draw sales.

Richard clearly came to this point in his career with plenty of drive and enthusiasm for making products with timber. But the core competencies he has been describing — the capabilities on which his business depends — are a little broader than these. They include managing a network of relationships with hardware and garden supplies outlets, the ability to source inexpensive materials and add a lot of value to them quickly, and running an effective distribution process.

He acknowledged that at peak times he had to work very long hours, much of it in the 'doing' activities (making the products and attending to their distribution). He was not yet at the point of substantially increasing the size of the business, but clearly he was already thinking of the steps involved — new product lines, the possibility of satellite manufacturing centres in other parts of the city to reduce transportation costs, and so on.

> As to the personal implications — I am not earning what I used to earn yet, but the other rewards are much greater. Healthwise, I have dropped 15 kilos, I have gone from taking six tablets a day for a bad back to taking none. I am enjoying work, rather than feeling I had to go. We do get trapped in corporate jobs, in part by the knowledge, in my case and that of others, that you have a partner and a young family to support and you can't put this at risk. I am now spending a lot more time with the family. They can see changes in me for the better.

The discussion with Richard which produced these comments occurred some six months into his new venture. I rang him again a few months afterwards. However, this time the voice answering his factory telephone said: 'Oh, Richard isn't here right now. In fact he has had a serious accident and is at home...'

I rang Richard at home and his first comment was: 'Hugh, if you are ringing in a break from one of your workshops on self-employment, talk to the group about disaster insurance!' Richard had run his hand through a band-saw at work. He had lost part of one finger and severely injured several others on the same hand. This was a major disaster for this fledgling business and it had occurred in the lead-up to Christmas, with all its attendant high volumes of work.

On the positive side, in the immediate aftermath of this incident, his full-time and casual employees had stepped into the breach and kept his business going. On the negative side, pre-Christmas sales increases were not achieved and, more importantly, Richard received a painful lesson about the need for disaster insurance.

Ten months later, I spoke with Richard again. What was he now doing? How was the business travelling and what had he learnt in the next period of running his own business?

Richard's business was pretty active and he was in the process of trialing new products. He had a new upmarket cubby house design, styled after a country cottage (with a verandah!), garden arches, a modular garden planter boxes and benches made in redgum. He had one or two other sidelines, one of which was fabricating hand benches for hand therapists. Not hard to work out where that idea came from.

Some problems had developed with a former full-time employee and Richard's staff now comprised two part-time employees. The new recruit had been hired through an organisation called Job Focus, which specialised in placing people with disabilities. Richard's new employee had a mental disability. Richard understood that the disability was susceptible to stress, but that his employee was also capable of self-management to some degree. In screening the candidates, Richard had been impressed with this young man's TAFE record, which attested to good carpentry skills. Job Focus would have supplied training support for up to three months, but it quickly became evident after two weeks on the job that this was not necessary. The new employee was doing well two months after starting and would be able to work more than the current three days per week if Richard's work volumes became sufficient to sustain this.

In an aside, Richard remarked that one of his challenges currently was keeping work up to two good staff in the factory.

Richard had been too busy to realise two early ambitions — participation in the House and Garden exhibition in the Exhibition Centre, and a satellite operation in the northern suburbs of Melbourne.

I asked Richard what he had learnt in the past ten months. It was a question asked with notice and, for the most part, Richard responded with fairly practical lessons.

I learnt that when times are tough in a business, it is easy to put off the regular disciplines such as recordkeeping and then find it twice as hard later on to have to address these lapses in focus. It is hard to be motivated to do these things when you are in survival mode and yet they are absolutely necessary.

I also learnt that you simply have to make time for development — in my case development of new products and new markets. I left some of this a bit late and some of the ideas I am now putting together should really have been in the market a month or so ago.

I also learnt that I had to make sure the desire to help people did not overshadow the need for good business sense. This was a reference to some difficulties with a former employee, where perhaps earlier and more decisive action would have been more appropriate. It is good to help people and this is one of my values, but it is important to not allow this to reach the point of significant detriment to the ongoing viability of your business.

I have learnt the value of building a strong reputation with customers. For example, I strive to deliver against customer orders within 24 hours. This contrasts with the one-week delivery cycle of my predecessor and has earned me terrific respect in my customer base.

I have also learnt the value, again in building customer loyalty, in tailoring my products to meet their customers' needs. If a customer wants something special built, say for an oversize dog, or whatever, I will always try to do it. My neighbour in the industrial estate where my factory is located assembles special transmissions for Porsche racing cars. In fact, he is the world wide supplier of these things. Arising from a conversation with him one day, I now assemble special crates for him as another small sideline.

I have also learnt that I need to keep abreast of external changes — changes in regulations, wage levels and the like. You can easily become detached from these things in the 'busyness' of running a small business.

There were some other things to emerge in our conversation, which I found equally interesting. Richard has regular Saturday breakfasts with a much older businessman who has become something of a mentor.

He is someone who appears to take great pleasure in my success. He provides encouragement and enthusiasm and is a good sounding board for some of my plans. If I had a major strategy, or change in business in mind, I would definitely test the ideas with him.

Richard conceded that he was prone to spending too much time in the 'doing' — building products himself, making deliveries and the like — and not enough time working on 'the business'. But these Saturday breakfasts provided a little time for stepping back and thinking about the bigger picture.

Richard had a picture of the business in mind for two years ahead. He hoped by then to be managing revenues approaching $500,000 per annum. The business would have a broader range of products, it would still deal through retailers rather than retail direct, he might own his own factory rather than be paying rent and he might by then have a supervisor, or operations manager, to free himself up for more activity in customer relations, product development and marketing.

He might also by then be more discriminating with customers, building up those with whom the relationship was more synergistic and dropping off those who carried one line only and for whom volumes and stock levels were unprofitable. He also thought he would keep small groups of staff focused on particular product lines, rather than have everyone able to build all products.

Having noted these aspirations, I didn't get the impression however that Richard had a business or financial plan setting out the steps involved, with the assumptions and the cash flow projections consistent with bringing this vision into being. This may be unkind. Richard did concede that he had a bit of a weakness in the area of financial analysis.

Without 'leading the witness' more than necessary, I probed around some of the other areas of our competency model. What was it that sustained Richard in the period following his accident?

I hate failure. I get frustrated when something does not go right. I did not want to let my family down. Some of it is pride — I did not want someone else having to step in. I did not want to be among the (high) statistics of small business failure.

If we turn back to the sharper competencies associated with self-employment, we are seeing here — and in other elements of Richard's story — illustrations of tenacity, discipline, maturity and self-confidence.

We returned to the motivations behind the new products being trialed, such as garden arches.

> I don't believe people like me should hang on to traditional products too long. We need to identify gaps in the market, send what we can do to fill them and then get in and produce to those market opportunities. I think it is a case of always being alert to where opportunities might lie.

This demonstrates resourcefulness, creativity and flexibility, listening and research skills.

In his work with his new employee:

> I have tried to give him confidence and encouragement rather than negative criticism. I have taken him out with me in the utility doing deliveries a few times, really to get to know him better one-on-one, to be able to learn about his situation without seeming to probe in front of his workmate. You can see him tense up with others [who question him directly]. I always try to get close to my staff, to give them the feeling that mistakes are OK if we set out to learn from them.

Influencing skills, integrity and again listening skills. Also illustrated is the much more fundamental competency of empathy — that vital ability to understand and work with the feelings of others.

Richard also demonstrated plenty of the fundamental competency of effectiveness with people in his account of how he builds customer loyalty.

> My relationships with customers are a critical business asset. I learn from them what they see as future new products and opportunities.

This is a form of ongoing concept testing.

> I set out to build trust with them—and I decline to do ongoing business with those who are exploitative or who don't reciprocate in the business of trusting each other.

Richard and I both felt that if there was a 'gap' in his repertoire of skills and competencies, it was in the area of analysis. He needs perhaps a little more than his Saturday morning sounding board here, someone who might help him construct some basic forms of contribution analysis, so that he can evaluate the true costs and contribution of each product line and customer. The same resource might also help him project alternate business scenarios leading to the vision of his business in two or three years time, so that Richard can spend appropriate time on the key building blocks of his chosen pathway.

Of course, finding a resource to help in this within the fairly narrow financial capacity of this business might be difficult — but here Richard could consider an accounting student who might be able to combine assignments with some short projects of value for the business.

Richard has a great deal going for him in terms of our model, with the possible exception of a gap in analytic skills. He will probably move to cover this as he finishes building the core manufacturing capabilities in the business and the process of testing new product lines.

## Summary

These are, of course, two stories among the many thousands possible. They were chosen because at first glance each person had a strong sense of independence. Trevor had built his career independently over some 20 years, managing some significant transitions in focus during that period. Richard was just beginning his new 'career', but with plenty of determination to succeed independently following many years in a corporate structure.

In both cases, the fundamental competencies of independent capability are illustrated. The sharper, derivative competencies associated with success in self-employment have also been revealed.

The next chapter reviews the recent careers of some people who have tried new fields of work altogether — although the distinction between them and these stories is a fairly fine one.

# *chapter eight*

**Creating new work**

Success in creating a new business requires a focus on unmet needs in the marketplace. An entrepreneur will ask: What are the solutions being looked for by businesses or people and how might I stitch together my talents and some resources and meet them profitably? This new work may not be provided by existing businesses and it may not be contained in the envelope of a 'job'. All sorts of examples are occurring around us in new added-value services, and in many of the businesses which are now franchised.

The services industry abounds with examples of new businesses catering for the too-busy lives of those who are employed. There is an increasing use of home cleaning, home laundry services, nappy washing and childminding creches. Lawnmowing services are becoming full 'garden design and house maintenance' services. There are now meal-cooking services and dinner party preparation services, home administration (bill paying, domestic accounting, even tax and investment management) and animal exercising services. Home delivery of groceries using Internet ordering facilities is taking off and pre-prepared meals are now sold to supermarkets by specialist suppliers and onsold to busy professionals. New franchises in this burgeoning sector of the economy include Dial-an-Angel, Dinners Done, Spit Roast Catering and Jim's Mowing.

Phil Ruthven, from Ibis Business Information (a business forecasting service), estimates that four million Australians are employed in household service organisations. 'In five years time, there will be only three reasons to mow your own lawn — you find the task therapeutic, you're an idiot or you can't afford to outsource.'[58]

New services organisations are also springing up to meet the needs of organisations. Installing and maintaining information systems, managing energy and telecommunications usage and managing call centres are just three examples.

---

[58] Phil Ruthven quoted in 'At Your Service.' in *Australian Financial Review*, 4–5 July 1998, p. 30, in the Small Business section.

## Three case studies in 'new work'

What sort of people take these plunges? What does it take to go out
and initiate a new service or product and build a business from it? This
chapter has the stories of three people who have done it.

Our focus is on those individual competencies which seem to be
called upon. How important are the 'titanium' qualities of resilience
and durability? Do these individuals illustrate independent capability
and do the paths each chose allow for the development of these
qualities?

### Paul McKessy

Paul founded a remarkable organisation called Breaking the Cycle. The
organisation 'recruited' jobs for long-term unemployed young people,
then enrolled eligible young people, trained them over an intensive
four-week period and subsequently supported them for another 12
months in their initial employment. After some six years, the
organisation helped take around 1200 young people off the dole and
into employment, with around 80 percent of these sustaining their
employment six months after the intensive training period was
completed.

The organisation has had to cease operations recently, having failed
to win a tender for ongoing work with unemployed young people
from the Australian Government. (There is a another story here. A
very effective and highly successful organisation has been sacrificed in
a process which reflects no credit on the bureaucratic agency which ran
a new centralised tender-evaluation process. However, this is not
germane to this book.)

For the time that it operated, the organisation combined a number
of elements in achieving desired outcomes, including a challenging and
innovative training program in which were embedded a range of
particular values and philosophies. Much of this was attributable to
Paul's vision and determination to find better solutions than those of
the welfare model in working with disadvantaged young people.

Breaking the Cycle believed that what it did in transforming the
lives of so many alienated young people each year was of major

significance in our communities. The drive from Paul and the staff of the organisation came very much from a sense of passion about what young people do and don't need and about the failure of the welfare system to address the particular aspirations and the unrealised talents of its clients.

Someone, of course, had to pay the bills. Suppliers and buyers had to be found for what the organisation had to offer and an income stream had to be created. Breaking the Cycle had to operate like a business, with at least some surplus of income over expenses. The ostensible market for this organisation was governments, who seek to move as many unemployed people off benefits as they can. The organisation had, in the past, negotiated fees from the Federal Government (primarily), which paid fees for agreed outcomes. The agreed outcomes were successful transition off benefits and sustained employment for the young people involved.

Employers comprise another possible market for organisations of this type. Many organisations are themselves keen to address the growing problem of the long-term unemployed. At the same time, they need young people with positive attitudes and a desire to succeed in employment. This is exactly what Breaking the Cycle achieved with its graduates. Governments have traditionally been very unsuccessful in delivering effective services to employers and a part of Breaking the Cycle's attraction to government agencies lay in the energy it brought to enrolling employers in the task of job creation.

Breaking the Cycle came into existence not only as a worthwhile charitable venture, but as a business, with primary customers in governments and employers. It was formed as a company limited by guarantee, operating with all the disciplines of a regular business. This was the work which Paul created, for himself and for growing numbers of trainers and other staff in the enterprise.

Paul began his career by dropping out of school and commencing an apprenticeship as a motor mechanic. He did not complete the apprenticeship, but went back to school after a period delivering bread and another period as a labourer stacking bricks. Paul then moved to youth work as a street worker, in conjunction with undertaking a diploma of community relations at Victoria College.

For a few years he worked for several groups in this field before going overseas backpacking for two years. On his return, after managing a refuge, he joined Melbourne City Mission, managing a multi-faceted community program in South Melbourne which attracted corporate and wider support. After some years in this environment, Paul broke away and over six months or so, with no salary or other financial support, founded Breaking the Cycle. After pilot programs with young people, the organisation was formed into a company — partly to help attract the participation of more regular businesses.

Paul is an intense and passionate individual — passionate mainly about 'doing things differently' in a way that succeeds for young people. He is a classic 'developer' and ideas person, but someone whom he acknowledges needs others about him to wrestle with the details and managerial aspects of his enterprise. He is intelligent and very eclectic, without being highly educated in a formal sense. He has good political instincts and an ability to engage others in his endeavours with young people.

Paul has had his share of setbacks, with some disastrous personal investments costing him and his family a great deal. Breaking the Cycle also had a turbulent six-year life, as Paul and his colleagues wrestled with cash flows, demanding government contracts and a wide range of employers. At the same time, Paul's indefatigable spirit carried him through these events and was certainly the driver of the terrific outcomes which Breaking the Cycle managed to deliver.

### Yolanda Pettinato

Yolanda has a portfolio of interests. She is a one-person 'business'. Her main activity is running weekend seminars in goal setting, personal planning, achieving fulfilment and self-actualisation. Her subsidiary activities include yoga classes and meditation training in a program called 'A Balanced Life', and managing the property investments which comprise her 'superannuation'.

Yolanda's customers include those in full-time professional occupations, full-time parents and people in a range of occupational mixes and circumstances.

In describing the courses, Yolanda said:

It is much more than how to manage your life. It is about knowing what is possible and how to go about achieving this. It is about removing the obstacles from your path to enable you to move forward with accountability, responsibility and maturity. It is also about health and fitness, family, friends, love and feeling happy inside with continuing contentment and keeping focused.

Yolanda also still has speaking engagements arising from an earlier, highly successful career selling income protection insurance and superannuation products and services.

Much of what Yolanda Pettinato does in the course of her business stems from her life beyond the jobs and studies which she has undertaken. Yolanda was the youngest of six children of Italian parents who came to Australia in the 1930s. All six children were born in Australia. In an unusual event for an Italian family, when Yolanda was nine months old her mother left the marriage and her family.

Yolanda and the next eldest sister were placed in an orphanage and when she was three, the eldest sister joined them. The three girls moved through three different orphanages until, when Yolanda was aged seven, they rejoined their father upon his marriage to another Italian woman. At this stage, she also met up with her brothers, who were then aged 12, 16 and 20.

My father took on another woman to be his wife. She was very hard and tough, and we felt as if we were her slaves. My father was like this too. He was from Calabria and had run a fruit business there successfully — but was now unsuccessful...

My father was also incestuous with me until I learnt how to manoeuvre myself away from him. I was very frightened of him as he could be very violent. We all had to leave school at 15 and get a job. We then had to bring back our pay packets and give them to him unopened. He was not educated and did not care for his children to be educated either. We never had a book of any description in the house. We were discouraged from going to school and we were not allowed to participate in any sports or school activities and even to do our homework. For a long period he was a market produce grower of vegetables and he preferred that we work in the fields rather than going to school.

At the age of 15 I left school and went to work. I found a job in a department store and two months later my father had a heart attack and died. In many ways it was the biggest relief of my life as it had become unbearable living with him and my stepmother in the house... on many occasions he threatened that he would kill one of us. I'm sure he would have done so had he not died.

However, after he died the household in a rented Housing Commission property fell apart and my sister and I were on the street. We had nothing but the clothes we wore and we relied on handouts and assistance from the Catholic Church and from others. We boarded with a number of people and eventually took on our own flat. We could only just cover the rent and outgoings with our wages. Second jobs (waitressing or kitchen work) were a must if we wanted any extras such as clothing or money to go out.

I had low self-esteem because I had a very bad speech impediment: I stuttered badly. I had never had any therapy for it, even at school. No-one cared. I only went to second year at High School. However, as I folded clothes at the counter in this lingerie shop, I used to envy the people who sat in the office. I decided to go to night school and learn how to type. As soon as my typing was good enough I applied for a job as a typist. To begin with, all I was given was filing work — so I kept moving on to different jobs and climbing the ladder to better and more challenging work.

Then one of my bosses invited me to be his Personal Secretary — but to do this I had to learn shorthand. Then I became an Executive Secretary. I did this right up until I was about 25 and then I left Australia to travel the world.

I had learnt money management skills very young. When I married I looked after the money matters and I saved everything. I had a second job, too, and saved from this. We were able to buy our first house at a very young age. However, the marriage did not work. When we separated, I cashed in my 50 percent of the assets and invested carefully. This money represented the beginning of my now quite substantial property portfolio.

Travelling the world was my education and I revelled in it. I lived in a nomadic way for about four years, with travel in the US, Canada, Mexico, Europe, China, South-East Asia and Japan — where I taught English for six months. When I returned to Australia, I realised that I did not know too much of this country either, so I lived in various states for a time. I waitressed and did temporary office work, and managed a restaurant in the snowfields at Thredbo.

Then I met a guy who believed I would be very good in sales. He was an insurance broker and because I had worked in an insurance office in a secretarial role I knew something of the work. I thought: What have I got to lose? I said to him that I would give it a go provided he did not put any pressure on me to sell products I did not want to sell. I would only sell those I believed in.

Within a year I was his top salesperson. I was selling income insurance and I really believed in it. I became well known in Australia for my success in selling and I was flown around Australia to speak to meetings of agents. I sold for a number of insurance companies during this time. My growth and exposure was rapid. I had no training in sales, but I believed in the product. I could only sell ethical products and I had to believe in it to achieve this success.

I started my own business — still in insurance sales. I set up a company called Financial Agency Services. I sold this business after 13 years. I was very successful, making at one time a salary via commission earnings of around $150, 000 each year.

The road after this was pretty tough.

Yolanda married again and continued to work and earn well. However she then lost much of her savings in the process of supporting business ventures of her husband, whose business at one stage faced the threat of bankruptcy.

I had to work very creatively — we were in the middle of the recession. I kept thinking about ways in which to earn more money. I had broadened my skill base to selling superannuation as well as insurance products. But in the course of this, I realised that what a lot of people needed was basic training in financial planning. I was helping people a lot at a very basic level, in budgeting. I decided to run financial planning seminars for women. I did not make a lot of money doing this but I would run them every month without fail. But it kept me focused — or provided a focus. Rather than worry about where I would get new clients from, I would run these free seminars. All I had to do was find new people to come to the seminars — and this (in turn generated a lot of business in insurance and superannuation).

Then I started charging fees for the seminars. I had a fee-based business as well as commission earnings. The seminars became self-generating.

I also decided to join Rostrum as a part of overcoming some lack of confidence and to improve my speaking ability. I also put myself in the firing line to become club secretary. For a year I had the weekly responsibility of preparing and reading the minutes. In doing this I, of course, had the empathy and support of the other club members. At the end of that year I had so much more confidence, as well as listening skills and the ability to take criticism. The process involved ongoing exposure to being criticised. I could prepare a speech and read out loud.

When I came to delivering my own seminars, I was already fairly confident. I could control my stammer and I knew how to make jokes and so on. In this period, someone nominated me for the industry award — the award of the life-writers association. It looked further than sales performance, covering mentoring, ethics and so on. On reading the material regarding the award, I decided to go for it. I was the only woman nominated for the award and I won it.

Because of this I was asked to speak at lots of conferences — to hundreds of people. I became better at speaking and I used to get standing ovations.

At this time I was teaching people to manage their money, at the most basic level sometimes. I began to realise that no matter how much money people had made, they would not succeed unless they had a clear focus in their lives, unless they had a clear direction in their lives and unless they felt good about themselves, they would have no money at the end of the day. I kept referring people to other courses I had done — and I had done many in my life.

I then designed a broader focus workshop, addressing personal growth and planning, integrating the many things I had learned in my life and from the courses I had done. The workshop was successful at a level that I could not believe. It was called 'Personal Planning'. I just could not believe how well it was received.

I had a chance to study and become more qualified in financial planning — the industry now requires accreditation. I had none. But I went away to a health farm and thought about things. I had got over my financial problems and left the [unsatisfactory] marriage, and I needed to choose my next direction. I decided that the planning workshops were the most rewarding thing I had ever done and I would build these up.

It is now a two-and-a-half day course — two days with an evening a week later. It is called 'Powerful Planning'. My customers are all referrals or people I meet through speaking engagements. Most come through referrals: at the end of each course, I ask participants to refer people. What they get in the course is that no matter what has happened to them in their lives, they can have a very happy life if they choose, and I show them how. I teach them skills to get this — they walk away with tools, real tools, to help them to achieve this outcome.

I have learnt these skills and tools from my own life, from watching other people and from numerous books and from the many, many courses I have done. It is much more than how to manage your life — it is about knowing what might be possible and how to go about achieving this. It is much more than about setting goals. Along the way we discuss the issues of accountability, of responsibility, of maturity, of achieving balance in health, fitness, family, friends and love... It is not just about setting goals. It is about feeling happy inside, feeling content.

The course takes 12 participants at a maximum. I cook for it — it is very holistic. It gets people on track and focused... If people have become victims, or feel betrayed or that life owes them something, it gets them over this. It gets people over broken marriages, it gets them over monetary problems—not by providing a magic wand (I am very clear about this), but by teaching them how to approach life. It teaches them how to create their own mission.

I run these six times a year. There is a lot of preparation for each weekend and a lot of work involved. I also do counselling after the course to individuals. The course provides a foundation. I won't counsel people who have not done the course. This provides income, too, but as a follow-on to the major work in the workshops.

The teaching I do in yoga and meditation is a separate business and this course is called 'A Balanced Life'. Generally, most of my clients from this activity also attend the 'Powerful Planning' workshop. This is a regular weekly or twice-weekly process for the individuals who come. It is not a 'course' as such. Everything I do is about achieving a balanced life — mental, physical and spiritual—and deepening these aspects.

I asked Yolanda how she might characterise a 'successor' for her business. (In her case, as with Trevor previously, I was using this question as a way of seeking her view of the competencies she deployed in her work.)

The person would have to have done my work: to have been enrolled in my program; to have at one point been a client; and to have a deep understanding of what I do. The person would have to in no way watch a clock and to be flexible in using time. They would have to have an attitude which is expressed in a quote I use : 'People don't care how much you know until they know how much you care.' The actual business [I do] comes from caring. If you care enough then the business comes to you.

There would have to be [in my successor] a like-minded philosophy to life. This is the focus on achieving balance in mind, body and spirit. They could not possibly do this work if they were unfit or drank themselves stupid. They would have to be very disciplined, because I am very disciplined.

This would be essential. They would have to be willing learners — with an open, lateral mind. They would have to be passionate about this work — and I mean passionate. They would need to have a level of personal independence — you could not be a doormat to do this work. They would need emotional maturity. This is what I teach. Separating fact from fiction.

## Steve Adamek

A completely new and quite different business has been developed by Steve Adamek. Steve had a 25-year career in the Australian banking industry, which he began in a clerical role soon after leaving school. He moved through a number of different areas of banking, reaching a senior professional level. In the ten years prior to his retrenchment, he was engaged in corporate and project finance, with close involvement in a range of syndicated limited resource project financings, of up to US$1.75 billion. The projects had a strong resource focus but with breadth across infrastructure and pipeline transactions. It was quite specialised work and the challenge for Steve was what he might do when this work was brought to an end by his retrenchment.

Steve is a family man, with four school-age children and he lives in an outer suburb of Melbourne. Most of his training has been in the world of banking but it included completion of the Chartered Institute of Company Secretaries Corporations Law course. He does not have a tertiary degree.

Steve is a quiet individual of some intensity who talks vigorously when the conversation is about his professional interests. He has a prodigious capacity for work.

At the time of his retrenchment and in the process of working through an outplacement program, Steve reflected on his experience, transferable skills and the opportunities or unmet needs in the marketplace. He reasoned that there were many smaller and medium-sized businesses which needed project financing just as much for their growth as did the larger businesses with whom he had been working. The barrier many faced was in accessing lenders, in preparing necessary documentation, in achieving the best terms and, most of all, in meeting the substantial fees charged by merchant banks and financiers.

He put together a proposition for target clients which went like this:

For you to achieve your growth opportunities you need to borrow, say, $1 million to $5 million. What I can do for you is sit with your staff for a couple of weeks and using your data prepare an information memorandum, prospectus (if needed) and any other materials through which financiers might assess your standing and the risks involved. I can do this in your offices with you.

I can then move out and negotiate on your behalf with a number of potential lenders and secure for you the best possible terms. I can then prepare the necessary documentation as will satisfy your lawyers and their lawyers — at a fraction of the cost that either group would charge you. I can do these things for you at a modest hourly rate, with then a small percentage of the borrowing as a success fee.

Steve put together some simple materials to support this proposition and to establish his credibility and began approaching a number of smaller mining and resource businesses. Within a very short time, he had a number of assignments. In the first year of his operations, his gross revenues exceeded six figures and the business continues to grow.

Steve did find, of course, that projects of this kind do not emerge in a steady flow and to sustain a more even flow of income he has developed a range of adjunct financial services, including trade finance advice and structuring, project evaluation, loan administration and risk management. He has broadened his client base to include non-resources companies.

Project financing entails a focus on cash flow. You move away from the more traditional accounting approach, with its emphasis on the balance sheet and an analysis of historical data. From the perspectives this entails, I am able to see things in a business which lend themselves to improvement. While I might have been there for one purpose — capital raising — I find myself typically able to add value in all sorts of ways, looking at systems improvement, administration costs, the disaggregation of the separate revenue streams and costs of businesses, and more as well.

Sometimes I end up as a 'transition manager' in a company — one which is going through an expansion phase. I might be selling under-utilised assets, reconstructing parts of the business, installing new procedures while major change is occurring in the business. This work outside the resources sector is mostly in small to medium-sized manufacturing businesses.

Steve explained that he sets out to win business through networking at business breakfasts, speaking at Rotary functions, and through some articles published in business journals. He acknowledged, though, that much of his work arises through referrals and through clients he has assisted in the past.

Clearly creating work — work which will meet needs of customers and generate income in a sustainable manner — calls on solid reserves of tenacity, creativity and self-confidence. The path through such a career is rarely straight, nor without substantial bumps and pot-holes. One of the issues faced by many people setting out to be self-employed is the implications it raises for the family.

Steve certainly felt that the confidence his wife had in him in his move to self-employment had been important to him. But at the same time, he acknowledged that working at home did produce some tensions and strains, especially during school holidays.

It is sometimes difficult for the children to understand that while I am at home, I am in fact 'at work'.

You tend not to disengage — you are always thinking about work. In fact, you need to enjoy your work so much that a separation of 'work' and 'pleasure' is not necessary. It is not possible [to manage any real separation]... so you had better get plenty of fulfilment from your work.

Holidays are something that I actually have to force myself to take. It is a major effort to turn off the mobile phone for two weeks or so, but this is what I tell myself I have to do and I do it.

Since Steve left the corporate world for this path — albeit involuntarily at the time — it was interesting to record another observation:

I have no regrets about the decision to take this path — there are real rewards in it — but I do miss the camaraderie of the team which you get in a larger organisation. I am not a 'sprinter', but I am often forced to be one in the work I do for clients. I am more of a 'miler' by nature, preferring to work through situations more fully over a longer time. When I go into a business I can never be a full member of their team and, of course, I always have to move on...

## Independent capability and 'new work'

What of the question asked at the beginning of this chapter: To what extent do you need independent capability in creating new work for yourself?

Self-control and a belief in themselves and in the value of what they set out to do, has been a clear strength in each of the three people described here. Was this an innate characteristic in each person? I can't be sure. But in the latest 'career' each has adopted, each one has certainly created their own picture of their business and of themselves in their business and held to that perception. Yolanda has had some ups and downs in her life and Paul's passage through earlier careers has not been very smooth either. All three, however, have been resilient and bounced forward after adversity. Each has built on their experience with strong self-assurance.

Each person has clearly been highly proactive in seeing and developing an opportunity. In Steve's case, he took the circumstance of retrenchment as an opportunity, rather than regarding it as a problem and set about exploring and developing a new market for his skills. In Paul and Yolanda's new careers, the focus was rather more on the inner lives and abilities of the people they would work with — with Paul especially taking on a large challenge given the complexities and politics involved in negotiating funding from governments. There aren't many people around with the courage to initiate a business offering new solutions in the difficult area of supporting long-term unemployed young people.

Empathy and listening skills gave each person the insights with which to launch forth into their new ventures. One senses, particularly in Paul and Yolanda's stories, that each venture began following some years of observation and experience.

The first question for anyone starting up a venture is: Is there a real need (that is, a market) for what I plan to do? Are there customers who will buy what I have to deliver? The next and subsequent questions are around such issues as Can I do what is required?, What resources will I need? and so on. But in getting to an answer to the first question, it is important to be able to listen and observe carefully and usually this requires empathy.

Each has had to be effective with other people — in Yolanda's case, with individuals, in Steve's case with prospective and current clients, and in Paul's case, with employers, government officials and politicians and with young people and staff. There are very few businesses or careers which can be grasped and built independently without clear skills in relating to people.

Analytic skills are perhaps harder to prove in two of the people whose stories have been told in this chapter. Certainly Steve needs these every day when analysing the financials of his business clients and in developing opportunities for them. But was this competency fundamental in the careers launched by Paul and Yolanda?

A measure of it was necessary in the initial appraisal of how the business might work and in Paul's case, in assessing the interests of the many stakeholders involved in Breaking the Cycle's operations. However, Paul is the first to admit that detailed analysis of particular situations is not his strength and he is careful to find people with such strengths who will work with him. Paul is highly intuitive — and so, I suspect, is Yolanda. Both are bright people and both are highly eclectic, ready to take on any ideas and insights which will assist their endeavours.

Perhaps we might add a rider to the base competency of analytic skills: If you haven't got this one, but you are ready to seek out others who have this ability and listen to their advice, you will get by with the other four.

Some would argue that you can get by without strong skills in analysis if you are a highly intuitive individual — meaning someone who by inspiration and instinct seems often able to choose the right decision. However, intuition is not something easily developed and can be wrong as often as it is right. At any rate, our focus is on those competencies which we can strengthen ourselves in building independent capability — and I don't know of many ways to build intuition!

## Summary

These three people certainly compare well against the more specific competencies associated with self-employment: tenacity, influencing skills, integrity, creativity and flexibility, discipline, resourcefulness, commercial acumen, the ability to be 'hungry but not greedy', self-control and self-confidence, listening and research skills and clear professional competence in their particular fields.

Another question was asked near the beginning of this chapter: Would choosing to develop new work — choosing to be self-employed in a new enterprise — help to develop the competencies of independent capability?

The answer is clearly yes, but the risks in embarking in this direction without well-developed base competencies are significant. There aren't many protective organisational layers in self-employment and nor is there the cushion of pre-established cash flows and customer relationships. Mistakes in handling people, in making false starts, in poor pricing decisions, come home to roost very quickly in self-employment. But within this higher risk context — provided we survive in this career — we learn very quickly and we come to rely on and build the competencies of independent capability.

This chapter closes with a comment from Paul — raising a theme explored in the final two chapters of this book:

I think people need to have a belief in themselves, a belief that what they're doing is valuable and they ideally should love what they're doing and have a desire to do well. Without these ingredients, it's very hard to be successful, to reach your potential. If you haven't a belief in yourself, you will be working against yourself. It is a good starting point — to believe you are of value leads to adapting your own identity as a successful person. It's not just about ability — you can have all the ability in the world and muck it up because you're negative, you self-sabotage.

# *chapter nine*

## Unplanned career transitions

Assuming the competencies of independent capability can be developed, the future might involve moving independently and effectively through organisations and across boundaries between them and within them. Some careers might include periods in self-employment, including periods creating 'new' work and enterprises. Ideally, we will be in charge of these moves, designing them, learning what is required in them, practising the skills involved and deciding when and in what direction they will occur.

However, sometimes career moves may be triggered by events beyond the individual's control, and there will be an 'unplanned' career transition to handle. The essence of *The Titanium Professional* is that, whether a working career transition is planned or unplanned, we can remain in charge of ourselves. With our newfound competencies in place, we can anticipate and manage the transition.

What does this mean? Certainly it means more than keeping our chin up in adversity and moving forward with the light of achievement in our eye!

## On being kicked in the bum with a rainbow

A self-managed career is one where the individual has a series of pictures of the work and working life desired, perhaps five years ahead. (It is pretty difficult to capture all that might be required in a position or working role ten years out — too much can change.) Self-management entails observation, questioning, constructing experience, trial and error and always working towards your picture of what you desire.

People who are focused on the experience they want for their own career development tend to get it. Transitions for them are sometimes significant, but more often incremental.

'This is great in theory,' you might argue, 'but sometimes transitions are forced upon us when we least expect them. Restructuring, downsizings and all the other events which result in jobs disappearing come along. These things tend to make all this talk about managing our own careers seem pretty academic.'

Is it possible to reconcile losing one's job and searching for another with self-managing one's career and being independent and capable in the process? Absolutely!

The best description for the experience of retrenchment, one which wonderfully captures the pain and the opportunity is: Wow, I feel as if I have been kicked in the bum with a rainbow! People who can say this (maybe in more elegant terms) embody two of the elements of independent capability as a minimum. These are self-control or self-confidence, and proactivity.

There are all sorts of tips for managing transitions through what might at first glance appear to be the extreme adversity of losing a job. An early tip from the well-intended is to look for the opportunity presented rather than dwell on the disturbance involved. However, this skips over a few issues which need to be addressed.

This is the territory of one of the new professions in the changing world of work — outplacement, or career transition consulting. The essence of this consulting practice is to create a framework and a variety of educative and support processes through which people, with all their individual differences, might effectively manage career transitions.

## The steps of career transition

The typical phases of outplacement — processes which we may learn to manage for ourselves — are as follows:

1 stepping back from recent experiences and reflecting on skills, abilities, aptitudes, values and optimum working environments
2 building a picture of clear work capabilities and from a wide picture with new directions encompassed, narrowing the field to identify work targets which best fit a desired new career
3 researching possibilities and maybe learning new skills in the context of research and target qualifications, doing some 'discovery' relating to new forms of work in new organisations or new opportunities
4 preparing for marketing — resumes, letters, networking, dealing with recruiters, developing and testing business concepts with others
5 undertaking marketing — the most effective process by far is that of

networking, rather than any hard selling of yourself;

6 interviewing and appraisal

7 negotiating optimum employment arrangements and the commencement of your new 'career'.

The services of outplacement consultants embrace each of these areas, with the principal distinctions between them being in how long the services are used, in the quality of resources and instruments supplied, and in the professionalism of consultants and their depth of experience.

Many organisations now routinely provide these services to those who are displaced. They do so perhaps in recognition of the breach they have made in the ongoing contract implied in full-time work: 'As long as you perform well, we will employ you productively'. There is also recognition that many who are displaced from jobs will need active support in re-establishing employment. Progressive employers see these services for outgoing staff as a measure to reassure those not being displaced that their employer is not as heartless as might otherwise be assumed. It is a part of securing a strong internal and external reputation.

## Managing our own transitions

Whether we have this service offered to us, or must manage it ourselves, how do we best 'manage our own transition' when the event is unplanned?

For those who are independently capable, a road map such as that outlined in the 'steps of career transition' above might be sufficient guidance, but there are some skills and knowledge which can help. For those for whom the event is a rude surprise and possibly traumatic, some of what is discussed here will help with rebuilding the essential competencies of independent capability.

The phrase 'manage our own transition' has a deliberate connotation. It suggests stepping back from the 'doingness' of a former role, adopting a new set of behaviours and 'work' for the time of transition and perhaps conducting that conversation we continuously have with ourselves more thoughtfully. This is a time for stepping back and taking stock.

As William Bridges remarks in *Transitions*, every transition begins with an ending. We have to move into a period of not having a job, or, as he terms it, a period of 'fertile emptiness'. It is a period, Bridges suggests, in which we have to *disengage* (from old relationships, self-image and activities), *disidentify* (to loosen the bonds of who we think we are so that we can go through transition to a new identity), become *disenchanted* (not so much as to be disillusioned but certainly to look at the more objective realities behind former 'enchantments') and tolerate *disorientation* (certainly meaningful, but not always enjoyable).[59]

Grief and hurt and anger are often manifested during and after a retrenchment, especially for those with long service in an organisation. But in time, and for most people, it becomes apparent that anger does not serve us. Besides, many people have a little voice inside them saying: 'Well, heck, maybe this whole thing might be just a little liberating. Maybe this is a blessing in disguise...'

## Assembling a picture of our abilities

When the emotional impact starts to recede, the first step is to begin noting down information about your aptitudes and values, some criteria for environments (in terms of people and organisational settings) you will seek, and what might be termed your transferable skills.

Frederick Davidson's book, *Handbook of Executive Survival*, provides valuable guidance about this phase of self-appraisal.[60] Some excellent notes on broadening your picture of the skills you used in your last job and evolving a picture of skills transferable to much wider contexts are provided in a book called *Change Your Career* by Mark Lewis and Kevin O'Neill.[61]

---

[59] William Bridges, *Transitions*, Addison-Wesley, Sydney, 1980.
[60] Frederick Davidson, *Handbook of Executive Survival*, The Business Library, Melbourne 1991. See especially pages 27–34.
[61] Mark Lewis and Kevin O'Neill, *Change Your Career*, Council of Adult Education, 1997.

### Generating a direction and reflecting on your choices

Your next step is the task of generating new career options and new possible organisational settings. It is a time of more research and discovery. The process of refining one's capabilities follows — or at least we begin to think of the value we could bring to possible new roles and industries, and then further refining these thoughts to a narrower list of target jobs and organisations. Sometimes in this phase people step away from work they don't enjoy and have never done well. This is the time to seek perhaps a better alignment with what you are best at or care for most.

I was recently engaged in a series of discussions with a very senior marketing executive. He had built his career in a substantial international FMCG business. He had significant international experience in the US, and several South-East Asian countries, as well as China and Australia.

He worked through the foregoing phases of transition management and embraced the next phases (which are marketing and networking) brilliantly, with the result that he was in the 'closing stages' of discussions with three different organisations interested in his talents. Each had the prospect of building on his corporate career, leading to roles with international responsibilities.

However, at the same time, he had been actively working with a former colleague in the development of a management buyout of a free-standing subsidiary of the firm from which he had come. Just to confuse things further, another opportunity of a similar character had been brought to him — another subsidiary business which might be bought from the parent which was as attractive and as synergistic as the first. What should he do?

He was at a turning point in a career sense (to state the obvious). But we went on to review the very different rewards of each path and the different priorities each might present. On the one hand, he had the prospect of further movement up the ladder in the corporate world, with all the power, perquisites, associations and image involved. He certainly knew a great deal about the internal skills of survival and growth in such environments.

On the other hand, for self-employed entrepreneurs or owner managers, overt status and corporate power figure hardly at all in their thinking. For them, their hunger lies in the growth of the business, the success of their 'baby'. Many do not pay themselves much in the early stages of growing their businesses as focus is on retaining earnings to fund further growth. Successful entrepreneurs thrive on adversity and can turn their hands to operating, marketing, managing external issues, reviewing finances, negotiating, managing staff and more besides — mostly on the run with little time for the finessing and politics of larger organisations.

The critical issue for this marketing executive was to decide what would give him the greatest fulfilment. What would he like to look back on in five years time? These were very different paths indeed.

A notable feature in these conversations was the sense of excitement in the individual involved. The retrenchment of a couple of months ago was now history, but also it was the trigger for a terrific period in this man's life, an opportunity he was not going to forfeit. As Bridges puts it (perhaps a little dramatically): 'Take this opportunity to discover what you really want' and 'Think of what would be unlived in your life if it were to end today…'[62]

Few of us have highly successful international careers in marketing as a background. For some of us, especially those yet to develop their own sense of independent capability, it is a little more difficult to feel liberated.

Bridges again:

*New beginnings are accessible to everyone and everyone has trouble with them. Much as we may wish to make a new beginning, some part of us resists doing so as though we were making the first step toward disaster. Everyone has a slightly different version of these anxieties and confusions, but in one way or another they all arise from the fear that real change destroys the old ways in which we established our security. To act on the basis of what we*

---

[62] Bridges, *Transitions*, pp. 124, 126.

*really want is to say 'I, a unique person, exist.' It is to assert that we are on our own in a much deeper sense than we ever imagined when we were originally setting up shop as adults. That process only involved independence; this involves autonomy.*[63]

This is the nature of the conversation people in this situation need to have with themselves at this time. Each should be open to new thinking, ready to explore new work and new organisational settings, reflective about what each new opportunity might mean for self-realisation. People who have been retrenched need to provide themselves with encouragement. This, after all, is what independently capable people do in other forms of adversity.

When it comes to drawing a clear picture of what to do next, there is plenty of advice to be had via books, the Internet and from the outplacement industry. The processes of resume preparation, marketing letters and the like are well-represented in every bookshop. The key is to be focused on what has been achieved in a past career and on what can be delivered in the new roles and organisations targeted. We need to do this succinctly, as there is growing intolerance for verbiage in everyday business correspondence. A one-page resume and a focused letter that get straight to the interests and requirements of the person receiving them are invaluable.

## Marketing and networking

Marketing — in this context and in the pure meaning of the word — is not selling yourself. It is discovering where needs are and signalling solutions in the work you might do. It demands research, largely through networking, that uncovers areas of opportunity. Networking is simply asking questions of the widest range of contacts you can muster, approaching any and every person you can reach with questions about the work in their industry and their organisation, and about issues being addressed by them. It is gathering intelligence about emerging opportunities. It is not about grabbing people by the lapels and 'selling yourself'. Even as you gather intelligence, asking

---

[63] *Ibid.*, p. 141.

increasingly thoughtful questions, you are, of course, opening the eyes of others, and becoming someone people want to talk more to.

Networking creates work and uncovers opportunities. It taps the much larger employment market beneath that handled through direct advertisements. The hidden work market — reached through networking — is where in excess of 80 percent of the clients of Davidson and Associates in Australia, New Zealand and parts of South-East Asia find their next careers. Only around 20 percent of their clients achieve their outcomes through newspaper advertisements.

Networking is asking advice — a much smaller 'ask' than asking for help in getting a job. Asking for advice is a flattering experience for those approached. Good questions can reveal more about the intelligence and capabilities of an individual than assertions and a sales pitch. A process of discovery into new industries and new organisations is also intensely interesting. It sounds like a cliché, but gathering intelligence is demonstrating intelligence.

Networking should be supplemented with desk research — using newspapers, published materials, expert commentaries and the Internet, so that intelligence is built from other sources as well.

Networking also entails an exchange of value — providing reciprocal advice or information to others, perhaps at a later point. As we discovered earlier, networking is increasingly a way of creating relationships which endure across the (often temporary) structures in which we work. It is therefore a skill which goes way beyond a career transition phase in our lives.

Out of this process comes an interview — hopefully more than one — if you are looking for employment within an organisation: 'It is interesting that you should ask about our work in this area — because this is where we need a new person. In fact, I would like to talk more carefully with you about your own possible contribution'. Bingo!

## Interviews

Once more, there is no shortage of publicly available material on interview techniques. It should be sufficient here to make some fundamental points.

The key to a good interview is preparation. Anticipate likely questions and prepare points you would like to get across. In one way or another, most interviews will cover the following questions:

- What do you know about us? (Do your homework on the organisation!)
- Tell me about your major achievements, in the last job and before it
- To what do you attribute your success? What are you good at?
- What do you not like doing? What are you not good at? (This is a bit of a trap question, where the best tactic is to keep the focus on what you are good at by indicating how you have overcome weaknesses.)
- Tell me in some detail about the project you are most proud of. What did you do?
- Tell me about a project where you were not able to achieve all that you wanted. What did you learn from this?
- What do you think you might bring to us?

There is a key question an interviewee should ask, among others, in the course of the conversations involved: "How will my effectiveness be measured, in, say, 12 months time?"

Why is this critical? The answer to this question establishes critical expectations. It shows what the job is really there to deliver. Secondly, the question identifies the questioner as someone interested in delivering outcomes — which is a healthy signal to give. Thirdly, the question often brings into the open some vagueness in the prospective employer's expectations. It is surprising how often employers have not thought through exactly what outcomes they should be seeking from new appointments. This very vagueness can be your opportunity to suggest some measures of effectiveness of your own. Needless to say, don't ask this question until you think you might be able to do this — but the chances are that your suggestions will clarify the employer's picture of the role and build their esteem for you in the process.

Much more could be said about interviews, but the best mental perspective is to see them as an exchange of information and discovery on *both* sides, and to see yourself as a portfolio of experience and talents which may or may not 'fit' the role and the context. Interviews are an exchange, not a process in which you are a seller peddling wares.

The senior marketing executive we met earlier ultimately decided upon returning to a corporate role. But as negotiations continued, he came to me with the advice that a prospective employer wanted him to travel to several Asian cities to meet key executives with whom he would work. He asked me how he should prepare himself for each interview. What messages should he deliver about himself?

My advice was that rather than worry about messages, he should prepare a list of questions for each person, questions designed to uncover their needs and aspirations for their bit of the business. In addition, he might do a little research on business issues in each area. Both sorts of preparation were undertaken brilliantly. The interviews then became thoughtful dialogue on each occasion and my friend was soon in the new role.

## Forming a contract

Finally, we come to the process of negotiating terms. It is a time for taking advice, for stepping back and being open to new arrangements. It is not a time for undervaluing your potential contribution, but it may be a time for considering contract employment, consulting and/or more performance-based remuneration, since these forms of engagement are growing in frequency. Ideally, the perspective of both partners in this contract is: How can this work best for both of us?

## Independent capability in career transition management

These, then, are the mechanics of managing transitions from one job to another when an unplanned move has been thrust upon you. What makes for success? What are the underlying factors? How can independent capability be developed and demonstrated in these phases of your life?

Part of the answer to this lies in the work outlined in the foregoing paragraphs. If we *manage* our response to an unplanned job loss through the steps of career transition, we will develop some measure of the competencies, the attitudes and talents involved in surviving such transitions. If we behave proactively, addressing each phase in a disciplined manner, along will come the values and aptitudes associated with independent capability. Behaviour is often the precursor to effective thinking, to the inner skills of survival. This is partly what is meant by managing our own transitions.

Our talents and dispositions can be looked on as 'givens' — a function of heredity, upbringing, personality, identification with significant others, or responses to others, formal training and the like. Our self-concept is a function of all of these things. We can regard our inner selves as 'who we are and that is the way it is' — and of course much of what is unique in every person is the result of many experiences and influences.

However, we can also 'manage ourselves', in our behaviour and our beliefs, thereby fashioning more effective adaptations to what lies ahead. We can *choose* what we believe and we can *choose* our behaviour, including how we respond to stress and the unexpected.

There is a significant place for self-talk in this — in the inner conversation all of us have with ourselves all of the time. As many motivational speakers and 'gurus' in the 'transform-yourselves-and-become-whatever-you-wish' business have discovered, we do create our own experiences in terms of what we believe. Our identity is composed partially in terms of what we believe about ourselves and we can *choose* those beliefs.

This is a time therefore for positive self-talk, for eliminating put-downs and for quietly acknowledging all that we can do. If this is coupled with some energy and discipline in the preparation and discovery work outlined, then we effectively 'manage our own transitions' and build independent capability in the process.

This is also a time for being realistic in recognising what we are not and avoiding impossible tilts at quite unsuitable jobs.

While we are managing transitions and our own self-esteem, it is important, as Anne Kotzman points out, to be open to new experience, to accept responsibility for ourselves and to accept ourselves and our strengths.

In her book, *Listen to Me, Listen to You*, she suggests that there is a sort of continuous loop linking *thoughts*, *feelings* and *behaviours* in all of us.[64] It is a linkage which, with a change in any one of the three, leads us in a spiral downwards to loss of self-esteem, or upwards to the building of self-esteem. If we initiate change in any of the three variables — whichever is most easy to change at the time — we can work on our own self-esteem. This is the essence of self-control, the first building block of independent capability. People with this competency effectively manage their own thoughts, feelings and behaviours, rather than allowing themselves to be overtaken by any of the three.

Positive self-esteem underpins the freedom independently capable people feel in addressing transitions, which is freedom to explore new forms of work, new industries, new balances between work and the rest of living. A positive and contained view of themselves makes independently capable people more attractive to others in the process of networking and in exploring opportunities for work. They don't present as a quivering mass of anxieties!

## Summary

The following table summarises some specific competencies associated with managing unplanned work transitions. Just as in self-employment we need sharper-edged competencies than the broader ones discussed in the wider context of this book, so too in handling such things as retrenchment another, sharper set of talents are needed. These have been crystallised through my experience, though I acknowledge the influence of a short article by Keith Warren.[65] Keith also has exposure to outplacement work and was summarising skills he associated with success in the people he worked with.

[64] Anne Kotzman, *Listen to Me, Listen to You*, Penguin, Melbourne, 1989, p. 13.
[65] Keith Warren, 'Seven traits mark the successful job seeker,' in *HR Monthly*, April 1997, p. 30.

## Table 9.1 Competencies for managing career transitions

| Competency | Meaning |
| --- | --- |
| Self-awareness | The ability to assess individual strengths and weaknesses with honesty and objectivity. Ability to capture and summarise achievements and bring out broad capabilities. |
| Emotional objectivity | Ability to see that you are not being singled out and to see the wider forces operating in your situation. Ability to build and gain through relationships, in which there is self-disclosure, reciprocity and mutuality. Ability to experience and manage the emotional reactions to being without a job. Preparedness to let go of anger. |
| Receptivity and flexibility | Being open to support from others and being open to learning and change. Tolerance of ambiguity and uncertainty. Listening skills and empathy. |
| Contextual awareness | Ability to understand your place in the bigger picture, to see transformations in business and the way work is organised objectively. Ability to identify opportunities which suit your capabilities in different fields of work. |
| Business acumen | Being able to view your work capabilities as a product, understanding (changing) business imperatives, marketing yourself appropriately to where real opportunities can be developed. |
| Direction and focus | Viewing your search as a full-time job, being focused on clearly defined goals, being committed, disciplined, well organised, proactive. Having tenacity. |

| Competency | Meaning |
|---|---|
| **Perceptiveness** | Understanding how you affect others (especially recruiters) and modifying your style as needed. Using this opportunity to reflect on behaviours of the past which may not have served you very well. |
| **Constructive optimism** | The ability to maintain belief in your capacity to obtain a desired outcome. Treating change as an opportunity to design a new and better career rather than a problem. Not 'blaming the system', not assuming anyone 'owes you a job', accepting rejection in job applications positively. |
| **Creativity** | Willingness to explore new areas of work and work patterns. Ability to look at new working opportunities emerging from restructuring such as privatisation, new service sectors, new community needs. |

Of course, some of these factors overlap, and the parallels with the elements discussed in Goleman's book, *Emotional Intelligence*, are strong. However, they are set out almost as a form of self-score table under these headings to assist a bit of robust self-appraisal and self-management, should the occasion arise.

The meta-competencies associated with broad independent capability as developed in Chapter 2 figure strongly in Table 9.1 as well. As with survival and growth in self-employment, effective navigation of an unplanned career transition rests on being independent and capable and tests the underlying competencies involved in a stretching manner. The experience can be both liberating and empowering — if you choose it to be.

# chapter ten

## Becoming a Titanium Professional

*The Titanium Professional* assumes that we want to grow and to achieve things in our careers, including sufficient remuneration. It asserts that we need to develop capability in the work we do and that we want to become independent in the process, not captive within or dependent upon any organisation — and certainly not damaged or even destroyed in the event of unplanned transitions.

Independent capability seems even more important because of the way work and relations with organisations are changing. New kinds of work are emerging at a rapid rate, and some of them capture the imaginations of those who seek self-employment. *We* change as we move on in our lives. We seek different types of fulfilment as we develop different expectations of working life.

We have explored some case studies: stories of people who seem to exemplify independent capability in the world of work around us. One of the themes that has emerged through these stories has been the inner confidence that these people have in themselves.

This is the first key requirement in building independent capability.

## Self-esteem is a critical first requirement

In reflecting on the working lives of those discussed in this book, the most important attribute in each of their moves and responses to career shifts has been their level of self-esteem. This is not manifest in any one behaviour or practice, but is a pre-condition for the effective achievement of all that has been discussed.

All of these people believe in themselves without arrogance. When they make mistakes or set-backs occur, their inner conversation is something like: Well, my behaviour here has not achieved what was needed, I had better try something different. It's never: You moron, look at how you mucked that up!

None of our case studies has had a smooth path in the careers each carved out, but all have faced transition with quiet confidence in themselves. None has been sabotaged by inner demons holding them back with inner criticism.

Self-esteem is perhaps most critical in the difficult circumstances of a retrenchment, for example. But a measure of it could be seen in almost all the incidents and experiences related by our case studies. No-one was observed falling on their swords over mistakes or misdirections. No-one spoke of long bouts of depressive, negative self-talk. An observer would consider each to have plenty of resilience and inner strength.

Susan mentioned the importance of family in the foundation of our personality and our inner strengths, and our early upbringing has a major impact on how much we can respect ourselves. The greatest gift of parenting is to create self-esteem in young people. Moving from a negative perception of oneself — from a tendency to hold back, to denigrate oneself in that inner conversation in our heads, to a positive, self-affirming state later in life — is extremely difficult.

If we don't have any, building self-esteem can be difficult. It is a harder issue to tackle than most others, but it is the most important. It is the basis for independence in anything. Self-esteem is not going to deliver corporate success on its own, but it will offer insulation from the politics which periodically infect most organisational environments and provide balance in difficult times. Those who are unflappable in crises, whose self-concept is firmly in place and found adequate, who somehow or other manage to remain unmoved and unencumbered by the opinions and pressures of others, are always admirable. This condition of inner serenity is not a function of seniority at all.

Managing self-esteem is all about managing that constant conversation we have with ourselves. It means giving ourselves quiet self-affirmations, focusing on what we can do well, rather than on the things we don't do well, accepting there are some things we can't do well and working around this. The ability to value ourselves is critical in achieving a sense of independence.

Many highly successful people in corporate environments are low in self-esteem and drive themselves into the ground, working longer and longer hours. They are dependent on corporate recognition, on having a place in the board room and on status and the insignia of office. People involved in career transition counselling often have to help individuals deal with a real sense of grief triggered by the removal of a former title and organisational status. It is done by helping people discover the real and more valuable talents within them; by helping them build a more sustainable kind of esteem following loss of an organisational position. In other words, it involves helping people rebuild a measure of independent capability.

If resilient professionals are to travel independently through their careers, guiding their moves where they can and capitalising on opportunities where a move is thrust upon them, then they need *both* independence within themselves *and* the steady building of capabilities in the context of employment or self-employment. This is why the two words are linked.

## Adopting values and practices that build key competencies

The next key requirement in achieving independent capability is the ability and the willingness to manage oneself with a focus on what needs to be achieved or accomplished. Independently capable people seem to adopt, or internalise, those values and practices which in turn build the competencies we have discussed. We *create* our own competencies by implementing a range of values or disciplines in the way we behave.

In the case studies, the values and practices in the right hand column of Table 10.1 are clearly evident.

## Table 10.1 The values and practices of independent capability

| Key competency | Operating values and practices |
|---|---|
| Self-control and self-management | Belief in yourself and an ability to not be dragged down by self-criticism. Absolute honesty with yourself and others. Taking charge of your own development and training, learning by doing, being unafraid of making mistakes. A disciplined focus on learning and on the development of solutions to difficulties. |

| Key competency | Operating values and practices |
| --- | --- |
| Initiative/proactivity | Self-direction and an ability to take risks and a measure of courage. Looking to prompt and lead change rather than waiting upon the actions of others. Having an inner sense of direction. |
| Empathy | Respect for others growing from the respect you have for yourself. Thinking hard about the views and experience of other people. Accepting and seeking to understand the feelings and emotions of others rather than being quick to make judgments based on your own experience and beliefs. |
| Effectiveness with others | Appreciation of group processes and the identity individuals gain in groups. Ability to lead by giving others ownership of decisions and actions. Achieving effective influence with others by being a good listener. |
| Analytical thinking | Being acquisitive for knowledge, with a readiness to collect and analyse data, thinking through its implications. |

One might debate which come first, the values and practices or the competencies, but people setting out to be independently capable *manage themselves* almost consciously, in terms of the values and practices on the right hand side of the table. In the process, they build or develop the key competencies of independent capability.

Even in the context of career transition and perhaps especially then, the self-management of these disciplines builds independent capability. If we *work* through the transition process, developing in ourselves a sense of purpose, inquiry and openness to the future, we build the competencies needed.

Here are a series of principles or imperatives, that independently capable people seem to follow in their working lives:

## Become the cause of your own experience

Independently capable people learn all the time by observing themselves as well as others. 'I decided I wasn't learning much in staying in that role, so I moved on — I wanted to develop broader skills' is the sort of comment heard often in discussions with our case studies. They were not moving on because something was unpleasant — in fact, independently capable people concentrate all the more on developing the abilities needed to turn such situations, or their response, around in difficult situations.

The phrase 'becoming the cause of your own experience' also implies adopting a desire to gain insights continuously. Some of us move through phases of work without learning beyond how to avoid boredom. Independently capable people look around all the time to learn along different dimensions.

In his discussions of emotional intelligence, Daniel Goleman gives primacy to the ability to control impulse — self-control. Self-control in turn hinges upon inner confidence. This competency is expressed in the ability to say to oneself as events unfold: 'Wait a bit — let me see what I can learn from this situation. I am a learning person.'

## Seize the day, most days

Each of the people discussed had initiated quite significant moves, in some instances a number of them, in the course of managing their careers. Each set goals — intentions of their own, not those led by others — then set out to fashion their experience and learning in the process. Paul's move out of secure employment to initiate a completely new organisation and trial a fundamentally new approach to dealing with long-term unemployed young people, was perhaps the most dramatic of the various initiatives taken.

We need to have the courage of our convictions, staying the course through set-backs as they arise, being proactive and opportunistic in the pursuit of our objectives. Each of these people seem to have an inner energy. Their various moves and experiences were largely at their own instigation, not that of the organisation they were within at the time. There has always been a goal or two actively guiding them.

We also need the ability to know when to accept that something is not going to work and to change direction without destructive self-criticism. Many of us drift, our moves and promotions largely directed by others. We might not set five-year goals or broad aspirations, we might not craft or design our experience, but independently capable people do.

## Listen, learn and respect others as much as yourself

Frank's recollections of an old-fashioned manager carefully documenting his requests of his team and his observations of Alan Jeans struck a chord with me. It reminded me of how many mentors and exemplars in my career seem to have been really great listeners. Their leadership was usually of the understated variety and always seemed to follow moments of intent listening, taking in carefully my concerns and perspectives before making a suggestion.

I once had a total tyrant of a manager, who was fortunately several layers above me in the organisational hierarchy. This person used to review the annual plans of a series of businesses within his domain, taking apart the numbers and assumptions with clinical precision, exposing weaknesses and challenging assumptions with quite awe-inspiring arrogance. He had a mind like a steel trap and his eye was inevitably drawn to the weak parts of our various plans.

He was replaced in time with a quiet American. The new regional head was just as intelligent and just as perceptive during the annual routine. However, the difference was in the new manager's approach. Typically, his questions about the same weak spots in our plans began with 'Help me to understand this bit of data over here...' We were not belittled or exposed to posturing, but to a quiet, respectful question or three. Needless to say, the second manager inspired far more loyalty and energy than the first.

The examples of this book demonstrate the inquiring position independently capable people take on almost everything. The approach with others, in any position and context, seems always to be one of: 'Anyone and everyone can teach me something — what can I learn from you..?'

### Learn how to lead and when to follow

Independently capable people have no difficulty at all shifting between the roles of leader and team participant when appropriate. At one time, Ian was leading an equestrian team in the Olympics, but back in his regular job he was one member of a department addressing a variety of internal and external issues impacting on an organisation.

Paul worked within a community organisation, broke away to found and lead Breaking the Cycle, and later stepped back from the role of Managing Director to focus on a role as a director and program developer.

Once again, we are seeing a measure of internal independence from the title each might have had in a particular organisation. Too often, people define themselves too tightly with an organisational position — and suffer significantly when that position is removed.

Part of independence is the ease with which independently capable people can move between leading and participating. This particular talent will be crucial in the emerging 'boundaryless' organisations described earlier, where at any one time an individual might be a member of one project team or perhaps two, and leader of another — where colleagues may be independent contractors or even employees of customer companies. Independently capable people move intuitively and easily through guiding and influencing and quietly delivering, without concern over hierarchy or formality, without the need of assigned authority and status.

### Look for the real facts and linkages, do your own analysis

Along with inner energy and a sense of direction in those who are independently capable, comes a continuing interest in acquiring knowledge. These people read widely and always seem ready to absorb new knowledge and to want to test it themselves.

A distinguishing practice in independently capable people is patience and tenacity in assembling and then looking at the real facts. Opinions flying about are taken on board simply as pieces of information, to be considered carefully along with any other facts gathered. Independently capable people draw their own conclusions rather than springing too quickly to those of others.

As well as looking at themselves when building independent capability, such people look carefully at what is happening in their organisations and beyond them to a broader economic or community context.

The Titanium Professional *has reviewed the way work is changing. The abilities and skills required of professionals and managers are changing significantly, through the influence of technology, globalisation, communications efficiencies, changes in organisation structures and employment relationships and in the expectations of new entrants to the working world. The old 'command and control' hierarchies are becoming obsolete and the imperatives and practices synonymous with 'good' management of past decades are no longer appropriate.*

Strategies for achieving independent growth in regular organisations were discussed, considering particularly the processes of learning about the key 'deliverables' of more senior roles and the self-managing projects which provide relevant experience. The importance of managing one's own career development rather than relying on those in the inner sanctum with their succession charts was also discussed.

We have taken a look at the very different context of self-employment, one which more and more of us need to think about. The particular attributes and talents which seem associated with success in self-employment were examined, as was the need to work in alliances with others who can cover gaps in our skills.

The stories of some people who not only branched into self-employment, but who created 'new work' were also explored. These people saw new opportunities to be serviced and constructed activities and services which would address the needs involved.

The operating values summarised here are certainly pretty critical personal orientations in the business of achieving independent capability. However, each context is different and we need to reflect quite specifically on what each requires in achieving our outcome.

Perhaps the most challenging situation as we work towards becoming independently capable is one in which we have lost our jobs. The particular variations of underlying competencies, which seemed of greatest value to cultivate here, have been explored.

Writing this book has been an exploration of a subject which has fascinated me for years. In thinking about the subject, it seemed to me that there are plenty of books on the subject of achieving independence and self-respect — some of the discover-your-inner-strengths-and-you-can-achieve-anything variety, and some seem more about disengaging altogether from the world of work and adopting unconventional faiths, aromatherapy and primal screaming as a form of self-realisation! There is also no shortage of guidance on how to be successful as a manager, as a sales executive, as a self-employed entrepreneur, with success measured more in terms of remuneration or in terms of achieving a position on top of a pyramid of one kind or another.

But the more central need to me was how one might be independent and capable in a broader sense than this, without being fixated on the next promotion. The need was to get to more than just 'survival' and to avoid dressing up as a more voracious, more aggressive 'corporate warrior' than the next person. Independent professionals need to address how they might replace a concern for job security with an ability to achieve career security. People seeking this condition (or outcome) also need to adopt practices which reinforce their inner security — their self-esteem, in the less certain, or less ordered, future world of work. When I adopted the metaphor of titanium, I was thinking of inner strength and durability, as much as the connotation of external resilience.

The need to achieve balance between many competing pressures has also been addressed. A proper balance between an investment of time in our non-work lives with our working roles, balance between doing many things concurrently and yet looking forward to what the next period of work (or non-work) will require and achieving a balance between being caught up in events and listening more thoughtfully to ourselves are all vital for our health, effectiveness and sanity.

Independently capable people will increasingly make choices about

how they will work and with whom they will work — quite
deliberately choosing their environments in the future. Certainly I
encourage those working through career transitions to do a thoughtful
'due diligence' upon the organisations they contemplate joining. Their
task is to assess the culture of the organisation carefully: the level of
collegiality, how strategy is developed, how customers are seen, how
learning occurs within it and how mistakes and changes in direction
are handled.

In the past we may have been a little too uncritical and perhaps a
little too ready to follow whatever lead is given. It is certainly
interesting to see young adults now opt in and out of different work
contexts as they reflect on the implications each career presents. But a
time does come when we have to opt *for* something by way of a career
and the building of capabilities — otherwise we simply won't achieve
the independence and freedom of a mature professional.

For those seeking regular employment, the employment contract of
the future will entail much greater reciprocity than that of the past.
Employers will need to provide a setting in which independent
professionals can learn new skills and talents — preferably on the basis
of the real projects for which they have enrolled. Communication will
need to be open and the demands of the organisation will need to be
balanced with a recognition of the wider lives all of us must live.

For the increasing numbers seeking self-employment — or
recognising contingent or project-based employment — relationships
will only be sustained between them and their clients (or temporary
hosts, in the case of contract arrangements) when there is again
candour, integrity and balance in expectations. People choosing this
environment for themselves will need to carefully marshal their
resources and be mindful of gaps in their talents. And they will need
tenacity, flexibility and energy in great quantity. Many will sustain
themselves in networks of like-minded small and sole-person
enterprises. Networking will be one of the fundamentals of sole-person
business survival and transition.

Finally, a point about values. I wondered at an earlier stage in the
book about the significance of values in independently capable people.

As we looked at the working lives of our case studies, high levels of personal integrity and humility seemed evident in each subject.

At one level, we are seeing a quiet resurgence of interest in values, or their absence, in organisational leaders. Through community concerns about the conspicuous absence of integrity in recent business leaders, through wider concerns about the environment and perhaps through the changing expectations of young adults, values are becoming more important generally. Business leaders are increasingly being challenged over ethical lapses, organisations held to account for their practices, and investors and customers demanding evidence of codes of practice and standards in the organisations with which they might deal.

Choices will increasingly be made by independently capable people to not join, or to remove themselves from, organisations with impoverished cultures and an absence of the important values. The decision to avoid these contexts derives from the fundamental issue of how we see ourselves *from the inside*. It is certainly hard to maintain true self-esteem if we are callous in our treatment of others, 'flexible' in our application of standards and lacking in integrity. It is not so much that we should be honest, compassionate, concerned for community issues and the like as a moral imperative, attractive as this may be. It is more that to be independently capable we need to have a framework of values respected by others and ourselves, in terms of which we build and sustain self-esteem. I am sure this is true for the majority of us, despite the example of the conspicuous few who seem to lack important human values, yet rise to dizzying heights.

This book has been written to analyse and promote the achievement of independent capability in work, to distill the essential elements and then to celebrate them in case studies. The central message is that we can manage ourselves and the steady creation of the competencies which underpin independent capability. We can do this in the varied contexts we have explored with some refinement of the competencies involved. We achieve independent capability through healthy self-esteem, through the adoption of the operating values and practices summarised above and through observation and analysis of the changing nature and context of work.

How 'high' we rise in our careers is not entirely another issue, but it has not been the primary focus. You can be liberated, resilient and independent as a professional in a variety of careers without attaching yourself to someone else's picture of seniority. Your own conception of yourself and your career is what matters.

# *Appendix 1*

The bulk of this book was first drafted during 1997 and 1998. In late 1998, Daniel Goleman's sequel to his first book on emotional intelligence was distributed in Australia. It was titled *Working with Emotional Intelligence*.

In this later book, Goleman sets out to discuss the five 'meta-abilities' which he now believes make up emotional intelligence. These are:

- self-awareness
- self-regulation
- motivation
- empathy
- social skills.

The parallels with the five elements which I concluded made for independent capability are extremely strong. Mine, you will recall, are:

- self-control and self-management
- initiative/proactivity
- ability to empathise
- effectiveness with others
- analytical thinking.

Goleman's first book clearly helped me crystallise much of my own thinking and I hope I have properly acknowledged my indebtedness to him. His second book also builds heavily on his own direct work with the authors of so much seminal material on competencies: Boyatzis, Lyle Spencer, and staff within Hay/McBer. Goleman expands the five 'meta-abilities' mentioned above into 25 particular competencies. For example, under 'self-awareness', he discusses the particular competencies of 'emotional awareness', 'accurate self-assessment' and 'self-confidence'. Under 'empathy', he discusses the particular competencies of 'understanding of others', 'developing others', 'service orientation', 'leveraging diversity' and 'political awareness'. I won't cover all 25 here. It therefore is a much more detailed exposition of the subject of emotional intelligence than I have attempted.

The focus of his second book is also more towards organisational life and towards achieving success within organisations and in fashioning them. My own focus has been more towards the individual and more in the direction of building *individual capability*.

In a discussion of the competencies underpinning leadership, he refers to a study he commissioned Hay/McBer to undertake, and their finding that the majority of the key discriminating competencies were those of emotional intelligence. (These included influence, political awareness, team leadership, self-confidence and the achievement drive.) The exception was that:

*just one cognitive ability distinguished star performers from average: pattern recognition, the 'big-picture' thinking that allows leaders to pick out the meaningful trends from the welter of information around them and to think strategically far into the future.*[66]

The parallels here with my fifth building block for independent capability — analytic ability — are certainly strong. There is little discussion in his later book of just what 'big-picture thinking' comprises. However, this certainly reinforces my own conclusion that four key components of emotional intelligence, together with a measure of analytic ability comprise the foundation of independent capability.

---

[66] Goleman, *Working With Emotional Intelligence*, p. 33.

# Bibliography

Alberici, Emma, *The Small Business Book*, Penguin, Melbourne, 1995.

Bermont, Hubert, *How to be a Successful Consultant in Your Own Field*, Prima Books, US, 1997.

Bridges, William, *Jobshift*, Allen & Unwin, Sydney, 1994.
— *Transitions*, Addison Wesley, 1993.

Briggs Myers, Isobel and Myers, Peter B., *Gifts Differing*, Consulting Psychologists Press Inc., Palo Alto, 1980.

Boyatzis, Richard, *The Competent Manager: A model for successful performance*, John Wiley and Sons, New York, 1982.

Covey, Stephen, *The Seven Habits of Highly Effective People,* The Business Library, Melbourne, 1990.

Davidson, Frederick, *Handbook of Executive Survival*, The Business Library, Melbourne, 1991.

De Bono, Edward, *Lateral Thinking for Management,* McGraw Hill, London.
— *Master Thinkers Handbook*, Penguin, London, 1990.
—*The 5 Day Course in Thinking*, Penguin, London, 1967.
— *Six Thinking Hats*, Little Brown and Co, 1999.
— *Lateral Thinking: Creativity Step by Step*, Harper Collins, 1990.

Ellyard, Peter, *Ideas for the New Millennium,* Melbourne University Press, Melbourne, 1998.

Friedman, Thomas, *The Lexus and the Olive Tree*, Harper Collins, London, 1999.

Gerber, Michael, *The E-Myth*, Harper Business, US, 1986.

Goleman, Daniel, *Emotional Intelligence*, Bloomsbury, London, 1996.
— *Working with Emotional Intelligence,* Bloomsbury, London, 1998.

Hakim, Cliff, *We Are All Self-employed*, Berrett Koehler Publishers, San Francisco, 1994.

Hames, Richard David, and Callanan, Geraldene, *Burying the 20th Century*, Business & Professional Publishing, Sydney, 1997.

Handy, Charles, *The Empty Raincoat*, Hutchinson, London, 1994.
— *The Age of Unreason*, Business Books Limited, London, 1989.

Johansen, Robert and Swigart, Rob, *Upsizing the Individual in the Downsized Organisation,* Century, London, 1995.

Kotzman, Anne, *Listen to Me, Listen to You*, Penguin Books, Melbourne, 1989.

Letcher, Marcus, *Making Your Future Work*, Pan Macmillan Australia, 1997.

Lewis, Mark and O'Neill, Kevin, *Change Your Career,* Council of Adult Education, 1997.

Micklethwait, John and Wooldridge, Adrian, *The Witch Doctors,* Heinemann, London, 1966.

Moodie, Ann-Maree, *Small Poppies*, Prentice Hall, Sydney, 1996.

Naisbitt, John, *Megatrends,* Macdonald and Co, Sydney, 1982
— *Megatrends Asia,* Nicholas Brealey Publishing, London, 1995.
— *Global Paradox*, Allen & Unwin, Australia, 1994.

Ohmae, Kenichi, *The End of the Nation State*, Harper Collins, London, 1995
— *The Borderless World*, William Collins and Co, London, 1990.
Reichfield, Fred, *The Loyalty Effect*, Harvard Business School Press, 1996.
Senge, Peter, *The Fifth Discipline*, Doubleday Books, New York, 1994.
Spencer, L. and Spencer, S., *Competence at Work: Models for superior performance*,
John Wiley and Sons, New York, 1993.
Turnbull, Noel, *The Millennium Edge*, Allen & Unwin, Sydney, 1996.

## Journal/newspaper articles

'At your service.' in *Australian Financial Review*, 4–5 July 1998, p. 30,
Smart Money section.
Mark Abernethy, 'FCA Rejects Franchise Slowdown Claim,' in
*Australian Financial Review*, 13 January 1998, p. 18, Small Business section.
Colebatch, Tim, 'Business on the rise despite the fears.' in *The Age*, 29 May 1998, p. 3.
Connors, Emma, 'E-mail a beast of burden to business,' in *Australian Financial
Review*, Saturday, 25 July 1998, p. 4.
Drucker, Peter, 'The Theory of Business.' in *Harvard Business Review*,
September 1994, p. 95.
Hirschorn, Larry and Gilmore, Thomas, 'The new boundaries of the boundaryless
company.' in *Harvard Business Review*, May/June, 1992, p. 104.
Jacobsen, Dave, 'E-commerce: It's more than buying and selling online.' in
*Company Director*, July 1999, p. 49.
Littler, C. R., Bramble, T. and Dunford, R., 'Downsizing: a Disease or a Cure?' in
*HR Monthly*, August 1996, pp. 8–12.
Marchant, T., Critchley, R. and Littler, C., 'Managers on the Move.' in *HR Monthly*,
October 1997, pp. 6–8.
Muysken, Jan, 'Are your competitors just a click away from your customers?' in
*Company Director*, July 1999, p. 25.
Ohmae, Kenichi, 'Life in the Round.' in *Management Today*, September 1998, pp. 8–9.
Pristel, Simon, 'Training the key to future jobs.' in *Herald Sun*, 25 January 1997, p.18.
Twomey, Paul, 'E-liminating the deadweight.' in *Company Director*, July 1999, p 14.
Ryan, Colleen, 'It seemed like a good idea.' in *Australian Financial Review*,
17 January 1998, p. 25.
Warren, Keith, 'Seven traits mark the successful job seeker.' in *HR Monthly*,
April 1997, p. 30.

# *About the Author*

Hugh Davies' broad experience comes from 30 years in a variety of senior human resource management roles in Australia, Asia and the UK. His career has included 14 years as Director Personnel and Corporate Affairs for a large multinational, counselling senior executives undergoing career transition, and as chairman of a non-profit organisation that worked with long-term unemployed young people. In 1996 Davies established his own management and consultancy business, which focussed on assisting organisations to develop management capability.